SUMMA PUBLICATIONS, INC.

Thomas M. Hines
Publisher

William C. Carter
Editor-in-chief

Editorial Board

Benjamin F. Bart
University of Pittsburgh

William Berg
University of Wisconsin

Germaine Brée
Wake Forest University

Michael Cartwright
McGill University

Hugh M. Davidson
University of Virginia

John D. Erickson
Louisiana State University

Wallace Fowlie
Duke University
(emeritus)

James Hamilton
University of Cincinnati

Freeman G. Henry
University of South Carolina

Grant E. Kaiser
Emory University

Norris J. Lacy
University of Kansas

Edouard Morot-Sir
University of North Carolina, Chapel Hill
(emeritus)

Jerry C. Nash
University of New Orleans

Albert Sonnenfeld
University of Southern California

Ronald W. Tobin
University of California, Santa Barbara

Philip A. Wadsworth
University of South Carolina
(emeritus)

Orders:
Box 20725
Birmingham, AL 35216

Editorial Address:
3601 Westbury Road
Birmingham, AL 35223

The Myth of Guillaume

The Myth of Guillaume

Poetic Consciousness in the Guillaume d'Orange Cycle

by

David P. Schenck

SUMMA PUBLICATIONS, INC.
Birmingham, Alabama
1988

Copyright 1988
Summa Publications, Inc.

ISBN 0-917786-54-8
Library of Congress Catalog Number 88-60711

Printed in the United States of America

Acknowledgments

Written works, as anyone who has ever attempted one knows only too well, are the products of considerable time spent alone in one's chambers. This one is no exception, and it, like others, would never have been finished were it not for the indulgence of many. To the following, therefore, go these sincere expressions of gratitude: to my parents, Charles and Harriet Schenck, for their love and for providing me the means and the encouragement to pursue the academic life; to Gerry Brault for introducing me to Guillaume and for his unflagging support of all of my professional efforts; to the University of South Florida for release time for some of this work; to my wife, Mary Jane, for her love and encouragement—she who of all the critics of my ideas has been the toughest and best; and to my children, Tyson and Katie, for their patience outside those chambers waiting for the work to be finished.

Additional thanks go to Indiana University Press for allowing me to reproduce a diagram from *A Theory of Semiotics* by Umberto Eco (Figure II, page 44) and likewise to Dover Press for allowing me to use a diagram from Hans Reichenbach's *The Philosophy of Space and Time* (Figure IV, page 106).

—D. P. S.

Contents

Chapter 1:	Introduction	1
Chapter 2:	The Myth	7
Chapter 3:	Semiosis of the Myth	35
Chapter 4:	Time	61
Chapter 5:	Space	87
Chapter 6:	The Final (Re)Turn	113
Notes		119
Bibliography		127
Index		139

Chapter One
Introduction

THIS IS A BOOK ABOUT A MYTH, a twelfth-century myth concerning the human integrative process or the desire of the individual to shape his environment according to his own image. It is about the rich and captivating story of Guillaume d'Orange and his partly historical, mostly legendary epic deeds that are collected in the remarkably coherent cycle bearing his name. This is a cycle that critical assessment would appear to judge much more closely unified than either the King or Doon de Mayence cycles, but which has not, in my view, been examined with regard to the literary design that provides the most profound and far-reaching sense of coherence to what I take to be the six central poems of the larger twenty-four poem cycle: *Chanson de Guillaume, Aliscans, Couronnement de Louis, Charroi de Nîmes, Prise d'Orange,* and *Moniage Guillaume.*[1] Specifically, this book explores the structure of the "myth of Guillaume" in these six works, the way in which the myth is generated textually, and its temporal and spatial aspects. More broadly, what follows is about the shared "epic consciousness" which produced this myth and which guaranteed its manifestation across and throughout a six-poem "mini-cycle" that is clearly the product not only of many hands but of many minds as well.

That there can be such a thing as a shared epic consciousness or common mythic design raises several interesting points. It means, first or all, that multiple poets, *jongleurs*, and perhaps also copyists all shared similar ideas, themes, concepts, and values. This may not seem particularly strange, especially in a period of literary history where poetic individuality was not as evident as at other times, but it is notable if, as I intend to show, what is held in common is so similar that it would appear that a single mythic conception informed all of these poems. In fact, although each poem has its own "story" or serves as a separate chapter in the life of Guillaume, and although it is clear that our extant texts are by no means the product of the same individual, there is a remarkable unity of conception and execution of these poems from a mythic point of view. Whether or not this implies a conscious sharing of issues and values found in these poems is largely immaterial, I think, but it does reinforce the notion of intertextuality now widely discussed with regard to medieval literature. As Paul Zumthor has said in respect to the notion of intertextuality, the production of a text is the actualization of traditional givens where these givens exist in the memory of the poet and the group to which he belongs ("Intertextualité et mouvance," 10). Zumthor's notion of intertextuality has much to say about what may have happened in the production of the Guillaume Cycle poems. In this situation it very much appears that these texts actualized *des virtualités préexistantes* or common ideas shared by the group to which these poets belonged regardless of how widely dispersed this group may have been. The point is that the stories were widely known and transmitted. Thus the opportunity for the sharing and influencing of one text or version of a text by another was not only possible but highly likely such that a common conception can be seen in its various expressions. As Zumthor himself has noted: "Les divers moments [du processus de la production du texte] sont clairement perceptibles dans la tradition narrative des chansons de geste, spécialement celles du cycle de Guillaume,..." (10).

Guillaume scholarship is well over a hundred years old, much of it tending in one way or another to deal with questions of coherence or unity within the cycle no doubt because it appears so much more unified than either of the other two major cycles. Investigations in this area have included both historical/philological studies and more modern literary critical approaches.

Alfred Jeanroy was one of the first to take a broad look at this cycle. In "Etudes sur le cycle de Guillaume au court nez. II. *Les Enfances Guillaume, Le Charroi de Nîmes, La Prise d'Orange*: Rapport de ces poèmes entre eux et avec *La Vita Willelmi*," he examined the historical relationships between these poems. More recently, Madeleine Tyssens's *Les gestes de Guillaume d'Orange dans les manuscrits cycliques* has demonstrated the philological relationships between the works collected in the cyclical manuscripts. Tyssens's purpose was to work towards the possibility of establishing as true a text as possible by means of a thorough and systematic analysis of the manuscript tradition, but her work also clearly shows the overall physical structure of the entire cycle. Of course, the *Chanson de Guillaume* itself does not figure in the cyclic manuscripts, but it has been the subject of considerable philological study not only because of its beauty and because it is one of the very earliest epics, but precisely because its lack of compositional unity is quite obvious. Jeanne Wathelet-Willem's *Recherches sur la "Chanson de Guillaume": études accompagnées d'une édition*, which discusses thoroughly the probable history behind the single surviving manuscript, also establishes a hypothetical text completely regularized in all respects such as language and versification.

The more literary, critical side of Guillaume scholarship can probably be said to have begun with Bédier in *Les légendes épiques* with analyses of style and characterization. Most literary analyses date from the mid-forties, however, when Ernst Robert Curtius published the first of two articles entitled "Über die altfranzösischen Epik" and suggested that the *Couronnement, Charroi, Prise,* and *Moniage Guillaume II* were all composed under one design, the purpose of which was to castigate the weaknesses of the monarchy under Louis VII and to evoke a vision of Carolingian glory. Philippe-August Becker (*Das Werden der Wilhelm— und Aimerigeste*) also saw these four poems as an intended unity, but he went even one step further than Curtius and claimed that all of them had been composed by a monk of St. Denis around 1150-60. Furthermore, he identified these four poems as the "Guillaume cycle proper." While it is doubtful that anyone would embrace the idea of single authorship of these poems today, his view testifies to the great sense of coherence that is seen among the Guillaume poems. More recent critical approaches have been in the areas of structuralism and semiotics. Here, for example, Alfred Adler's *Epische Spekulanten. Versuch einer synchronischen Geschichte des altfranzösischen Epos* attempts to demonstrate the firm structural relationships existing between poems regardless of how intentionally or unintentionally they were related. Finally, Larry Crist's "Remarques sur la structure de la chanson de geste: *Charroi de Nîmes— Prise d'Orange*" has shown the close interrelationship between these two texts by means of a complex semiotic analysis.

These references to but a few of the many studies on the Guillaume poems offer a clear indication of the significant interest that has been shown in the relationship of the various poems to one another. But, as with Wathelet-Willem's exhaustive studies of the *Chanson de Guillaume*, there has also been marked concern to deal with unity or coherence in single poems of the cycle as well. Apart from the *Guillaume*, this interest has been directed primarily at the *Couronnement de Louis*.

In 1854 Wilhelm J. A. Jonckbloet published the first edition of the *Couronnement* and attempted to deal with the historicity of the various branches. Jonckbloet was concerned with such questions as whether the figure of Guillaume was a composite of various historical personnages, whether the coronation of Louis at Aix really represented the historical event of 813, whether Guillaume's first expedition to Italy represented that of Louis II around 873, and which rebellious vassals and uprisings are really represented by Guillaume's missions to Andorra, St. Gilles, and Pierrelatte. Such concerns may seem inconsequential to us today since it is now widely accepted that the *Couronnement* is clearly a composite embellished by legend, but Jonckbloet set the stage for work that was to come much later.

Bédier (*Les légendes épiques*) believed that despite the branch-like nature of the poem, the extant text showed evidence of a later redactor's attempt to give some semblance of thematic or logical unity to the poem, and he identified that unity as the overriding theme of Guillaume's defense of his lord at all costs. Alfred Adler ("The Dubious Nature of Guillaume's Loyalty in *Le Coronnement de Louis*") and Jean Frappier (*Les chansons de geste du cycle de Guillaume d'Orange*) followed in similar veins, the former suggesting that a continual struggle for the Holy Roman Empire and the latter proposing that the defense of Church and Crown were the major themes of this poem. Thus, despite the fact that the *Couronnement* reveals some obvious breaks in the narrative and that it has most likely been pieced together from earlier texts, there is strong feeling that it has thematic unity of some kind. In fact, although I have taken a different tack from that of others, it is precisely that belief which has inspired the work for this book.

Jean Frappier's comment that the *Couronnement* was an "épopée à tiroirs" caused me to look deeply into this poem (*Les chansons de geste du Guillaume d'Orange*, II, 116). My own first readings of the text, however, suggested to me that there was a clear and profound message in the work as a whole which has not been discussed. In my view the poem reflected a basic civilizing desire on the part of Guillaume, a desire expressed in archetypal terms as an attempt to give human proportions to nature or to the immediate environment. This was the conclusion drawn from the observation of a curious repetition of certain archetypal symbols and patterns of behavior that united the various branches. This civilizing drive appeared to me to be a more profound and central theme to the poem than any previously offered, such as Guillaume's selfless defense of Church and Crown. The latter theme is certainly there, but it is not, to my mind, nearly as basic nor as significant because it does not have the complex structure supporting it that the civilization theme does (see chapter two).

As a result of this observation, and mindful of Frappier's view that the *Couronnement* was the "chanson directrice" of the cycle (*Les chansons de geste...*, II, 17-18) and Tyssens's opinion that the *Couronnement, Charroi,* and *Prise* formed a "noyau cyclique" (*Les gestes de Guillaume d'Orange...*, 153-62 and 431-41), I examined those remaining poems which make up the poetic biography of the hero: *Enfances Guillaume, Chanson de Guillaume, Aliscans, Charroi, Prise,* and *Moniage Guillaume*.[2] The results were surprising, for except for the *Enfances* the same civilizing notion was found as the central focus for each poem. In examining other poems of this cycle and poems of other cycles, however, I found the results to be largely negative.[3] That is to say, there did not appear to be any consistent or coherent archetypal civilizing theme to the extent that it occurred in the six Guillaume poems with the exception of *Aymeri de Narbonne, Mort Aymeri de Narbonne, Les Narbonnais,* and the Guillaume section of the *Bataille Loquifer,* all of which form part of the larger Guillaume d'Orange Cycle. I am now satisfied that there is something very special about the six Guillaume poems offered for discussion here and that my studies allow me to draw the following conclusions: (1) that those poems dealing most closely with the life of Guillaume are all informed of a basic civilizing myth, (2) that the myth of Guillaume as civilizer testifies to a shared poetic consciousness of those responsible for our extant text, (3) that by virtue of intertextual borrowings this consciousness may have found its way to a noticeable degree into the three Aymeri poems and, not surprisingly perhaps, into the Guillaume section of the *Bataille Loquifer*, and (4) that the late addition of the *Enfances Guillaume* to the larger cycle as a means of rounding out Guillaume's poetic biography may have meant that it was far enough separated from the spirit of the other poems not to have been informed of the same structure.

The fact that I see the story of Guillaume as a myth has dictated the parts and orientation of this book. Chapter two opens with a discussion of myth from a general point of view, particularly as I see its relationship to the Guillaume poems in question. The structure and significance of the myth is then explored in the six poems. Chapter three is a consideration of the semiosis of the myth, or a detailed analysis of the way in which the myth is generated textually. I have chosen to explore the generation of the myth from a semiotic perspective because this is a very logical one in which to study the codes of myth. Then, because myths can only be fully understood if their temporal and spatial aspects are thoroughly explored, chapters four and five will deal with those issues respectively. In this way I believe we may appreciate a unique and profound literary statement of the early epic period of medieval France, one which has a great deal to say about the integrative process of the individual and one which ultimately gives humanizing form to this process in one unique, spatial, and timeless instant, that is to say, in the mythic image of Guillaume himself.

Chapter Two

The Myth

MYTH IS A COMPLEX SUBJECT about which much has been written with great diversity of opinion. In some ways it is an intimidating subject given the range of functions myths may perform and the various ways in which the subject might be approached, and the only proper place to begin is with a definition regardless of how tentative that definition may be.

Myth is an expression of the way things are.[1] By this I mean a statement in either imagistic or narrative form that reflects man's view of how things were prior to his arrival in the present moment, how they are now, or how man would like them to be. This definition is intended to embrace the possibilities of explaining origins, behavior, human desire, or value systems. It is also intended to include myths which may be given by a single static image such as might be projected by a single word as well as the more commonly accepted form of myth, that is to say one developed in a narrative. Thus, under this definition we might include such things as the Oedipus myth, Gilgamesh, Theseus and the Minotaur, the African Mwindo epic, Roland, or Christianity. All of these myths attempt to explain something about man's origins, his behavior patterns, or his value systems. And, all of them are capable of doing so in narrative form even though they may also occur before us in some imagistic form such as the Cross or a likeness of a mythic hero.

Under the definition suggested here the primary function of myth is to offer man a process by which he can integrate himself into his world, to solve problems of contradiction, to express his position in the world in terms acceptable to himself, and to satisfy his dreams and desires in some meaningful way. This integrative function is the most essential and fundamental part of myth. It is, in fact, the very reason for the existence of the myth, and it satisfies every notion of it that we are likely to encounter. It says simply that man's primary concern in myth is to become one with his environment, be it physical, social, psychological, political, or whatever, and such that he becomes a satisfied part of a whole in which answers to troubling questions may be given, in which conflicts or contradictions may be overcome, or in which he feels he has some control of his life situation. The result of such a concern, which is in fact the motivating factor underlying the primary concern, is the fact of the creation of the communicable myth, the "gestalt," the text. Giving form to the myth is therapeutic not only in that it allows man to work through a process or to become active in problem solving, but in that it also allows man to create a textual space in which he becomes integrated and is thus able to sublimate his integrative needs with respect to the real world. Moreover, insofar as it is in the text that answers are given, that problems are solved, and that integration is achieved, the text becomes the world of concern confronted by the powers of myth. It is thus that the myth becomes the extremely important and powerful expression of man's relationship to his environment, for there can be nothing more crucial than the ability to satisfy oneself with respect to the space of consequence in which one finds oneself. To the extent that the myth can actually express this space and man's relationship to it textually, there is nothing more elemental concerning man's expressive tendencies than the production of myth. It is small wonder, then, that primitive societies, or even more advanced societies engaged in early literary experiments, tend to generate large numbers of myths. Gilgamesh, the Mwindo epic, and the *Roland* are good examples of products of these types of societies in serious pursuit of resolving important questions concerning man's relationship to his immediate environment.

As indicated above, however, there is nothing simple about myth, and the most difficult part of dealing with it is determining how it functions or how it communicates its message and generates its particular form. If we examine the general structure of myth, three levels may be appreciated, each one found successively deeper within the text: (1) a narrative level, (2) a syntagmatic/paradigmatic level, and (3) an "emic" level.

In the first, or narrative level, we are concerned with the facts of the narrative or with the subject and the action of that subject. In the case of the *Chanson de Roland* this may be given simply as "Roland sacrifices himself for the sake of France and Christianity." Obviously, a great deal more can

The Myth 9

and needs to be said to describe this myth adequately, but the point is that in its simplest form the narrative need be represented by nothing more than an identification of the subject and its predicate.

The syntagmatic/paradigmatic level of myth is pivotal, for it is here that temporal and atemporal functions of myth meet, that is, those aspects which depend upon a chronological development (the narrative proper) and those which exist outside of time such as mythemes, archetypes, and motifs. It is also here that the two basic patterns of development of the myth appear: the linear, having to do with the flow of the narrative; and the circular, having to do with the ritual nature of the myth. This is the level where full semanticization of the myth takes place.

Primary semanticization occurs at the emic level.[2] Moving progressively deeper into the structure of the text we find mythemes, sememes, semes, lexemes, morphemes, and phonemes, each of which takes on significance because of its binary relationship to another mytheme, sememe, and so forth.[3] This is the level where we encounter those elemental units of the narrative usually identified as symbol, image, motif, and theme. These are troublesome terms, for there is almost never universal agreement on the definition of them. It is also essential that we be able to relate them to the various sublevels of the emic level. Let us attempt to distinguish first between image and symbol.

In *The Literary Symbol* William York Tindall defines an image as "a definite object, or at least as the semblance of an object, which, though nothing much in itself, has received import from experience and memory" (6). The symbol is "a visible sign of something invisible, a reference to something indefinite" (5-6). Later he refines his position a bit to suggest that "The image, like the symbol of which it is a principal kind, appears to be a verbal embodiment of thought and feeling" (105), but he notes that "A traditional image is either a natural thing, like a tree, or an artifact..." (125), and he says further that symbols must be more well defined by their context. Tindall's suggestions are a good place to start, but let us add our own refinements and adopt the following: that an image is an object that is projected into the visual space of a receiver such that he recognizes it immediately for what it is in any context. A symbol, then, is a concrete sign, an image of something abstract (e.g., a rose symbolizing love) but which must be defined by the specific context in which it occurs.

The terms motif and theme have probably been less well distinguished from one another than image and symbol. Most would agree that a theme is an abstraction, but while some also see motif as an abstraction, others will see it as something concrete, perhaps similar to a symbol or an image. In *A Handbook to Literature,* C. Hugh Holman has defined motif as "A simple element which serves as a basis for expanded narrative; or, less strictly, a conventional situation, device, interest, or incident employed in folklore, fiction, or drama" (329). He defines theme as "The central or dominating idea in a literary work" (528). Eugene H. Falk largely supports these definitions in *Types of Thematic Structure* by giving the motif as "such textual elements as actions, statements revealing states of mind or feelings, gesture, or meaningful environmental settings" and theme as "the idea that emerges from motifs by means of an abstraction" (2). The important factors here are that the theme is abstract and that the motif is a component part of the theme. Thus in medieval romance the knight errant, the lady, and the single combat all serve as elements of the theme of courtly love. It is easy to see how one might view these motifs as images or as symbols.

We must finally relate these terms of image, symbol, motif, and theme to the various aspects of the emic level of myth. Symbols and images find their origins rooted in lexemes which are in turn composed of morphemes and phonemes. Here lexemes are viewed as nothing more than unsemanticized utterances. As semes, or denotative and connotative markers (what may very loosely be called "characteristics"), become associated with these lexemes, we move up to the level of sememes or "concepts" composed of clusters of semantic markers. It is here that motifs (e.g., "knight") first become apparent. As this process of clustering and further semanticization continues, themes and finally mythemes emerge where the latter may be defined as the central or dominating idea of the myth. As the process progresses therefore from lexemes to mythemes, the various elements become less concrete and more abstract.[4]

Turning now to the myth of Guillaume, the integrative function spoken of above is found at the base of this myth and in all of the six poems in question. The myth of Guillaume is a way of looking at the world. It is a statement about how things are, or in this case about how they ought to be. It is an expression of how man attempts to become part of his world, to civilize it, or to give human proportions to it. The myth is expressed as an essential and repetitive pattern of behavior, but as the myth is developed through the six poems it also comes to be represented by the image of Guillaume himself. The hero thus becomes a mythic image representing not only certain static qualities but various patterns of behavior as well. This is to say that the image possesses both syntagmatic and paradigmatic properites like the narrative in which it is found. The significance of this will become apparent as the structure of the myth is explored.

This myth could presumably be analyzed from one of two directions: either by starting at the level of mythemes and working down into the text or by starting at the level of phonemes and working up. Neither is realistic, however, for in the first case we must presume that we already know what the myth is, a doubtful proposition since we can only be certain of it once we have analyzed all of its constituent parts, and in the second case we cannot be sure where an analysis of all the phonemes and morphemes would lead us (even if we wanted to undertake such a task!) knowing that not all of them will be used directly in the composition of the myth anyway. In fact, we are drawn to those repetitive elements which impinge upon our literary consciousness while allowing the unique structure of the text to evolve inductively from it, striving as much as possible to eliminate any preoccupations by trying to examine all incidents and their apparent supporting images objectively.

A close look at the action of the *Couronnement de Louis* reveals that while the hero is involved in battle after battle, he withdraws for a period of rest between one battle or period of work and another. Furthermore, it is during these periods of work and rest that the poet evokes certain images in repetitive patterns: *nature, water, fire, food,* and *wasteland.* These images are significant not simply because of their recurrence but also because of their constant signification. They may have either apocalyptic or demonic meanings in the sense in which these two terms are used in archetypal criticism.[5] That is, these images may suggest growth, renewal, and peace or well-being, or they may suggest the opposite.

The five images mentioned above serve as the foundation of a unique four-level structure informing the *Couronnement*. Above the images are found a level consisting of two basic themes, a level containing a cycle of action, and the final level or goal of the poem which we will express here as civilization (see Figure I).

Figure I

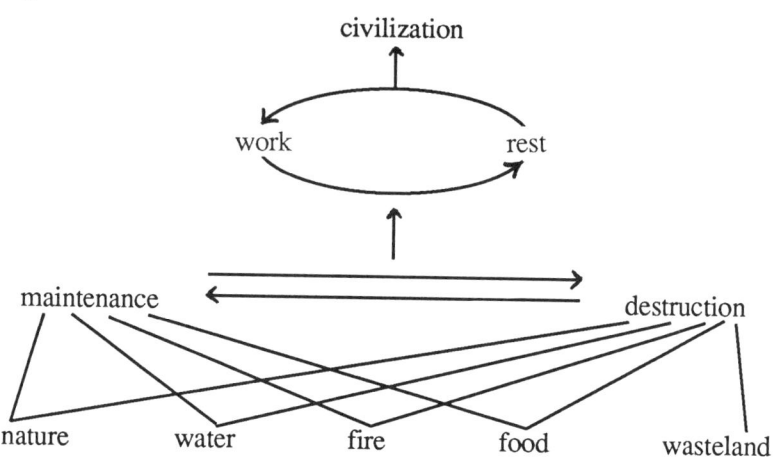

The images of Level I create either the "maintenance of the kingdom" motif or its opposing "destruction" motif depending upon whether they occur in their apocalyptic or demonic phase. All five images can exist in either phase with the obvious exception of *wasteland* which will generate only the "destruction" motif. The polar motifs then constitute the second structural level of the poem. They in turn provide the impetus for a "work/rest" cycle through which Guillaume must turn; this is represented by the third structural level which is the level concerning the action, the narrative proper. This cycle moves the hero toward his goal of civilization which will be suggested by the elimination of disruptive forces, the establishment of a strong and effective rule represented as Level IV.

The four-level structure is typically manifested in the following way: after a hard battle Guillaume retires to a natural setting (*nature*) where he relaxes and refreshes with *food* and *water*. The three images appear here in an apocalyptic phase for they evoke a motif of peace and renewal, or as indicated in Level II, a maintenance motif. Guillaume not only maintains his strength by retiring to nature and by refreshing with water, but at this point in the narrative he has also brought the kingdom once again to a stable situation which, in effect, he controls.

Contrasting with the maintenance motif is the opposite motif of destruction which is created by images in the demonic phase. New troubles begin with an enemy burning and laying waste to an area supposedly under the king's influence, and this new motif naturally calls Guillaume from his period of rest back to his usual work. Thus, the entire poem seems to be constructed upon a polarity constitued by the two motifs in a dynamic equilibrium, first one predominating, then the other. This suggests a natural phenomenon, the cyclical nature of human experience, a Wheel of Fortune. The significance of this alternation is that it naturally affects Guillaume who turns through a series of work/rest cycles in response to the actions of the motifs. His work, as we have already observed, appears simply to be that of defending Church and Crown. Yet such an interpretation of the poem demands that we see Guillaume's cycles of actions as based primarily upon the two opposing motifs, ignoring the underlying images which create them. There is no question but that images such as horses, knights, weapons and the like could constitute such motifs. These are the images we would expect to find in a defense of Church and Crown theme, but they do not appear to group themselves into any unique structure as is found with the five images of Level I. Guillaume therefore appears to be very closely tied to nature, and, as we will see, he attempts to remake his natural environment into his own image. Such is the stuff of civilization from an archetypal point of view.

The poem opens with a three-laisse prologue in which the scene is set: we hear that Guillaume has already suffered greatly at the hands of the Saracens; we are reminded of God's work in creating the ninety-nine kingdoms, suggesting that perhaps man must also work to restore unity to his world, that is, to acquire the final kingdom; and we hear that:

> Reis qui de France porte corone d'or
> Prodom deit estre et vaillanz de son cors;
> Et s'il est om qui li face nul tort,
> Ne deit guarir ne a plain ne a bos
> De ci qu'il l'ait o recreant o mort:
> (vv. 20-24)

The reference to natural loci in verse 23 might be taken simply as a figure of speech, but it is a curious one and already suggests that such loci are for rest and not for one who has work to do.

The story proper begins with Arneis's attempts to persuade Charles to make him regent until Louis is old enough to reign by himself. Guillaume, meanwhile, is on his way back to the palace when he appears from out of a wood. This is the beginning of the first work/rest cycle. We might presume Guillaume to have been in the rest phase of an earlier cycle as represented by the nature image of the wood, but he will now go to work to protect Louis, spurred on by Arneis who suggests a destruction motif. The work phase is in fact quite explicit, for as Guillaume says to the traitor upon accidentally slaying him:

> Tu le [Loois] deüsses amer et tenir chier,
> Creistre ses terres et alever ses fiez.
> (vv. 137-38)

Here it is clear that Guillaume is intent upon civilizing in terms of building or developing, not in simply maintaining a status quo or in protecting the king. His environment, particularly land, must conform to the image of man represented here by the king. Here again, however, the desirable motif spoken of by Guillaume is balanced by an antithetical motif of destruction. Charles instructs Louis that a good king must protect the meek and destroy the enemy:

> Tote sa terre guaster et esseillier.
> (.....)
> Ainceis li fai toz les membres trenchier,
> Ardeir en feu ou en aive neier;
> (vv. 192-96)

This motif of destruction is grounded upon wasteland, fire, and water images all in demonic phases. Or we might look upon the fire and water images as having cleansing and purificatory properties as we would find in apocalyptic imagery. Moreover, there is a food image in demonic phase where Charles counsels his son to "act like a man-eating leopard" before the proud (v. 187). Guillaume has been spurred into action by a desire to maintain and to build the kingdom as well as by the threat of its destruction, two motifs based upon the nature, water, fire, and food images.

As Branch II opens it would appear that Guillaume has again come full circle to his rest phase after the work of securing the kingdom from the threat of Anseis: he agrees to protect Louis, but as if seeking spiritual as well as physical renewal, he asks first for time to make a pilgrimage to Rome. Upon arriving at the city he is fed and allowed to rest. The following morning he hears Mass and receives the spiritual food of renewal. He is immediately thereafter paid a visit by the Pope who tells him of Galafre's seige of the city. The Holy Apostle promises Guillaume eternal rest in Heaven if he will first secure Rome. This marks the end of Guillaume's period of rest and it is the recurrence of the various images that recreate a destruction motif upon which the hero's work phase is established. Galafre blames God for his father's fiery death from a lightening bolt and boasts of his having taken revenge upon many Christians whom he has made to

> Ardeir en feu et en aive neier;
> (v. 533)

Furthermore, he threatens the Pope:

> Et tei meïsme, qui sire iés del mostier,
> Ferai rostir sor charbons en foier,
> Si que li feies en cherra el brasier.
> (vv. 541-43)

Guillaume counters twice that none of God's chosen people will be "burned in fire or drowned in water" (vv. 579, 587), and it is as if this little banter and the motif created by these demonic images really urge Guillaume into action. Yet while he is preparing for battle, so also is Corsolt who has a table prepared so as to take nourishment analogous to the Mass. Even the enemy's work is preceded by a period of refreshment and renewal.

Guillaume's work of maintaining and building the kingdom is about to begin again. This is immediately reinforced in the first of the long prayers:

> Glorios Deus, qui me fesistes né,
> Fesis la terre tot a ta volonté,
> Si la closis environ de la mer;
> (vv. 695-97)

Here, again, God is the creator, the worker. He is a figure emulated by Guillaume as the latter tries to create his own earthly kingdom. To support this image even further, Guillaume mentions Adam and Eve's expulsion from the Garden:

> De paradis les en covint aler
> Venir a terre, foïr et laborer,
> Et mortel vie sofrir et endurer.
> (vv. 704-06)

This is by far one of the most interesting passages of the poem for it re-emphasizes the reference to work in the Biblical account, making it clear that the Garden and the earth are two different entities and that man has specifically come *a terre* as if to work it, to carve his own world out of it.

Demonic imagery continues in the account of Guillaume's encounter with Corsolt, for Guillaume makes an insulting reference to the drunken Mahomet's having been devoured by swine (vv. 851-52) as well as to Jonas's having been swallowed by the whale (v. 1016), while Corsolt threatens to make provender of Louis and Guillaume (vv. 1101-08). In each case there appear both a demonic food image and a motif of destruction based upon it, a motif which causes Guillaume to enter a period of work.

Guillaume slays the giant and is urged to rest by Bertran:

> Oncles Guillelmes, faites vos aaisier,
> Car molt par estes penes et travailliez.
> (vv. 1175-76)

He cannot rest, of course, while a threat to peace remains in the person of Galafre. Accordingly, the latter is converted to Christianity and is reborn of the spirit with the Tiber serving as baptismal font. Here the water image suggests not only the theme of maintenance but the growth of the kingdom through this conversion of Galfre, Guillaume following his own advice to *creistre ses terres*. The new rest phase of Guillaume's work/rest cycle is then suggested by the meal in celebration:

> L'aive demandent, s'assieent al mangier.
> (v. 1293)

This Branch, and another cycle, comes to a close with Guillaume's reward of Orable's hand in marriage. The water and food images, as well as the impending marriage, suggest renewal, rest, and the growth of the society for which Guillaume works.

As is to be expected, the rest phase does not last long, for two messengers arrive to warn the Count that disorder again reigns in France:

> Tot le pais on a dolor torné,
> (v. 1401)

This wasteland image creates a new motif of destruction to which Guillaume will respond as before. Appropriately, it is Sunday, fifteen days after Easter, and Guillaume is about to begin a new life with Orable. But before that can take place, a new work/rest cycle will commence whereby the hero will attempt to offer new life and growth to the kingdom. He hurries to Tours where Louis is beseiged by Acelin. Upon surveying the situation Guillaume dispatches the messenger, Alelme, to offer a truce to Acelin, but the latter only responds with threats. Alelme hurries back to report to Guillaume and declares:

> Ne fust por ce qu'esteie messagiers,
> Il m'eüst fait toz les membres trenchier,
> Ardeir en feu o en aive neier.
> (vv. 1866-68)

The familiar formula naturally spurs Guillaume on to engage Acelin in battle, to slay him, and to obtain promise of fealty from his father, Richart. He does not rest at this point, however, but continues working for his lord by roaming three years over Poitou, securing the region from rebellious vassals.

He then leaves his men in Poitou and heads for Rouen where Richart bitterly swears vengeance for Acelin's death. The poet gives no apparent reason for Guillaume's solitary trip to Rouen, but we might almost guess that it is for a brief rest. In fact we find that the morning after his arrival he thinks of riding for Lyons but stops on his way:

> En une lande sont descendu a pié;
> Li païsant lor portent a mangier.
> Quant ont disné li noble chevalier,

> Alquant s'endorment, car il sont travaillié.
> (vv. 2087-90)

This should be evidence enough of the end of a work phase, but the poet reinforces it further with the report that Guillaume and twelve knights

> Sor la riviere se vont esbaneier.
> (v. 2101)

presumably for some friendly jousting, a diversion from their usual activity and yet a means of conditioning and renewal of skills, a renewal underlined by the symbolism of the water image. It is then that Richart and company disturb Guillaume, challenge him, and must be subdued. Guillaume's new work cycle ends when Richart is delivered to Louis's prison at Orléans at which time Branch III also ends.

We then hear:

> Or se cuide Guillelmes reposer,
> Vivre de bos et en riviere aler.
> (vv. 2223-24)

Woods and water are obviously a source of rest, renewal, and refreshment. Yet a new destruction motif is evoked upon arrival of messengers from Rome who report that the entire countryside there has fallen prey to Gui d'Allemagne. Guillaume heads immediately for Rome, and as if to seek refreshment before more work, he orders food prepared while he and his men go out foraging and laying waste to the countryside. This last act not only underlines the impending battle but is a chance for the Franks to gain refreshment through food. Guillaume then returns to camp, subdues Gui, turns him over to Louis, and returns to his foraging.

This new foraging expedition seems very much out of place here and can really only be explained in light of all we have seen thus far: Guillaume's work phase ended, he now returns to forage for food, an image supporting the maintenance motif and Guillaume's desires to reduce nature to human proportions, to make his environment his servant. Yet as we know, Gui refuses to be subdued and begins the attack anew. Guillaume responds as before, and in this new work effort slays the transgressor and throws him into the Tiber. Thus, the demonic waters of dissolution put an end to another threat to the kingdom as Branch IV ends.

Unsurprisingly, Branch V opens on a peaceful note structured upon:

> Or se cuida Guillelme reposer,
> Deduire en bos et en riviere aler;
> (vv. 2657-58)

Rebellious vassals, however,

> Les viles [de France] ardent, le païs font guaster,
> (v. 2662)

thereby creating a wasteland image where new work must begin again in response to the motif of destruction. The poem ends with Guillaume successfully securing the kingdom for an ungrateful Louis and the final work/rest cycle coming to an end. The poem also ends with the suggestion that the civilization goal has been achieved. Guillaume has certainly behaved much like the "typical" epic hero defending Church and Crown against the infidel. But, beyond that, he has done it through a close association with certain natural elements as if to suggest that civilization for him is defined in terms of these archetypes.

Guillaume's real task is to integrate himself and his people with their environment such that they may peacefully *vivre de bos et en riviere aler*. This is not to suggest that leisure or some "return to nature" ideal is the goal. The whole emphasis upon human work argues to the contrary. It is rather to suggest that hindrances to man's effective integration with his environment, hindrances such as Saracens and rebellious vassals, must be eliminated or converted into useful or harmless elements. In the *Couronnement* we have observed actions concerning impediments to a civilized Frankish world as heavily dependant upon five specific archetypes. Guillaume responds to Galafre's demonic threats of death by fire and water, and to Gui's threat of wasteland, by ultimately baptising the former and "dissolving" the latter; Guillaume converts the demonic into the apocalyptic, or forces his environment to conform to his image. Thus, we are dealing here with something more basic than a "defense" theme, although the superficial actions of the poem, the epic battles for the throne, may be seen as metaphors for the underlying structure.

The other five poems of our "petit cycle" are likewise concerned with an archetypal civilizing goal founded upon the efforts of human work and given impetus by the five archetypal images we have examined in the *Couronnement*. The structure, the occurrences of images and patterns of action, is not an exact copy of that observed in the latter for each of the other poems has its own uniqueness and individuality, but the general dependence of the civilization goal upon the five images, dual motifs, and work/rest cycle is maintained. Guillaume is not always seen to want to *vivre de bos et en riviere aler*, but he is seen to want to *creistre ses teres* by presiding over the defeat of the enemy and the conversion of important Saracens (*Chanson de Guillaume, Aliscans, Prise d'Orange*), or by insisting upon a unified kingdom and working for his own share in it directly through a food image (*Charroi de Nîmes*), or by giving human proportions to his environment (*Moniage Guillaume*). The poetic consciousness of the *Couronnement* is maintained even if specific manifestations of it may appear modified in the other poems.

The predominant images in G1 of the *Chanson de Guillaume* are water and wasteland with the former occurring primarily in its demonic phase.[6] The result is that G1 is of a strongly negative tone for the Franks and not just because they suffer terrible defeats during this part of the poem. The prologue itself evokes the wasteland motif with reference to the great battle that will take place at Archamps. This is then reinforced with the use of the *gaste* in the narrator's description of the devastation that Deramed has brought to Archamps, the messenger's report of the same to Tedbald, and Tedbald's own assessment of the situation upon sober reflection the morning after his drunken revelry. It can well be said that the overriding tone of G1 is one of impending doom with the lowest ebb coming at the very end of it where Vivien lies mortally wounded by the *duit troblé;* the wasteland image underscores and exacerbates this tone.

The water image is largely tied to the image of the Saracens having come from *halte mer*. It is less a question here of water as a means of dissolution, but rather as a source of evil and misfortune. Thus we hear that Deramed *en halte mer en ad mise la flote* (v. 13), that Tedbald *gardet es haltes eigues* (v. 150), that the enemy are everywhere to be seen, *e en mer e en terre* (v. 162). The Saracens in fact become so closely associated with the sea that the two images share each other's characteristics, and salt water comes to denote "evil." The sea is the haven for the enemy who will return to their ships after a battle or when under attack. Moreover, salt water itself plagues the Frankish defenders: the only water Girart has at his disposal as he heads off to summon Guillaume is *ewe salse*; and, Vivien has nothing to drink but the water of the *duit troblé* which he cannot keep down. While this suggests Vivien's inability to make the Saracen world part of himself, Girart and Guischard will later seek refreshment either from wine or the *duit troblé*, perhaps suggesting that the Franks will utimately overcome the Saracens, integrating some of them within the Christian camp. It is also clear that water boundaries mark the influence of the Franks as when Vivien reminds Tedbald that he is *mult honurez des meillurs homs de rivage de mer* (vv. 51-52), and when Guillaume states that there is no better vassal than Vivien *De ça le Rin, ne de dela la mer* (v. 1599), that is in either pagandom or Christendom. What is known, *Terre Certaine,* is good; what is unknown and beyond the waters is not.

Occurrences of other images in G1 are limited but follow the pattern seen in the *Couronnement*. Girart will be offered food and drink upon his return to the court, and Guibourc will see to it that food is prepared for a new army or for Guillaume upon his return. Likewise the Saracens will withdraw for food after the battle at Archamps where they are surprised by Guillaume's arrival. These apocalyptic occurrences of food will establish rest phases of the cycle, even for the Saracens. Girart and Guillaume, for example, rest before returning to work. And young Gui will even take a break from battle to regain his strength by raiding the Saracens' food. Thus, the familiar images are repeated in cyclic fashion in G1, but it is the demonic water and wasteland images that are primarily responsible for generating the action and advancing the narrative.

If G1 relies most heavily upon water and wasteland, G2 is the "food" section, especially with regard to Rainouart. It is in this part of the poem that things take a definitive upswing for Guillaume and his men, and this appears to be reinforced by the rejuvenating properties of food. As expected, Guillaume washes and is fed upon his return to Orange after his discovery of Vivien; even his horse is properly nourished. He is also fed upon his arrival at Laon when asking Louis for help as well as before departing from Orange for the last battle at Archamps, and it is clear that all during this time Guillaume is in a rest phase. Once we meet Rainouart, however, we come to associate the food image more with him, for he has spent his life under Louis preparing food in the King's kitchens, and he is quite concerned before agreeing to leave with Guillaume that he have enough to eat. During the ensuing battle he laments that had he stayed back at Laon he would now have plenty. Rainouart, in fact, becomes a food metaphor and serves to reinforce the maintenance motif of the poem. It is through this former kitchen knave that the Franks will be victorious at Archamps.

The real significance of Rainouart and the food image, however, becomes evident after the victory and the subsequent return to Orange. The Franks wash with water and sit down to eat—the maintenance motif and the rest phase are reaffirmed. But, Rainouart is left out of the festivities through an oversight—who would ask a kitchen knave to dinner, anyway!—and he swears to return to his pagan homeland *d'ultre mer*. Suddenly a great effort is needed in apologizing to Rainouart and persuading him to return, but return he does, and there is more washing and eating, which is then followed by his baptism. Thus, the poem ends on the apocalyptic images of water and food. Rainouart is converted and reunited with his long-lost sister, Guibourc, and the Frankish society is not only reaffirmed but increased by the addition of a new and powerful member. The former Saracen, like Guibourc, has been converted into a form with which the Franks can be comfortably integrated, that is, one of their own. The civilization goal has been achieved, and in this case it is primarily through overcoming demonic water images (G1) and in effectively utilizing the apocalyptic food image as represented by Rainouart (G2).

The *Aliscans* is one of the most interesting Old French poems and one which has perhaps not received as much attention as it should have. At over 8,500 lines it is one of the longest of the Guillaume Cycle, but probably neither its length nor the fact that the only available edition dates from 1903 have discouraged study of it. No doubt it has all too often been seen as merely a long version of the *Chanson de Guillaume*. *Aliscans* is indeed a doubling of the earlier poem, but it is rich in possibilities. The character of Rainouart is much more fully developed here than in the *Chanson de Guillaume*, and with the addition of the episode of the bean farmer, along with the general support of the four-level structure, the *Aliscans* again reinforces the archetypal civilizing notion of the other poems.

As in the *Couronnement* and the *Guillaume*, the prologue of the *Aliscans* evokes the wasteland image even though the word itself does not occur, and we find that the Saracens emerge from their ships on the sea. Water is again demonic, and it is clear that Guillaume's work phase is beginning. Moreover, the water boundaries are important here as in the *Guillaume*, for except for Rainouart there is said to be no one stronger than the Saracen Aerofles, up to the *mer betée*. The Rhine is also mentioned again as a frontier of Frankish influence. This demonic image occurs additionally in a reminder that the Franks are suffering near the sea and that Guillaume fears drowning. The same tone that opened the *Guillaume* is repeated here with one notable exception: the *duit troblé* has been replaced by an *estanc*, and it is here that Vivien comes for confession and here that Guillaume finds him and offers him communion. Clearly, Vivien will die, but just as clearly he is being cleansed and refreshed. The *estanc* also marks the end of Guillaume's brief rest phase, for he spends the night here before entering battle.

The projection of antithetical images will continue with Guillaume's return to Orange, but although the apocalyptic phase is suggested with his bringing food and drink back for the embattled city, it really does not signal a significant rest phase. Demonic images overbalance it. Guillaume describes for Guibourc the wasteland at the battle site, as well as how the enemy is burning and making a wasteland of Orange. Moreover, he adds that he must *cors traveillier et pener* (v. 1688) and that he will enjoy no earthly pleasures, neither food nor drink save the meanest of sustenance, while there is work to be done.

The poet then begins to weave a fine texture of contradictory suggestions concerning work and rest as Guillaume sets off for Laon to seek aid from Louis. The purpose of this is not only to maintain the structure established by the polar images, but also to prepare the way for the inversion of a demonic image in the person of Rainouart found in the subsequent divisions of the text. In the Laon section, Guillaume goes through Orléans and Estampes on his way to the court and naturally passes by woods and water on the way. Upon arrival at Laon, he is first refused entrance to the city, and although he is offered simple food and drink by Guimar, he can neither eat nor rest well while there is work to do. When he finally does gain entrance, the usual refreshments are shared with the images repeated several times for emphasis. The idea of renewal is reinforced with another meal that includes Guimar and his family. Guillaume is obviously in a rest phase, but this is carefully tempered all along by the poet's notation that Guillaume partakes only of simple food and cannot really enjoy it at this time. Moreover, there are suggestions of the demonic side of the food image where Guillaume scorns Blancheflor for her gluttonous eating habits and where those of Rainouart are likened to those of a "two-bearded *vilain*." Food is obviously for refreshment and renewal but only under the right conditions. There will be no luxury, no celebrations while work is left. Even Rainouart, whom Guillaume fears will not be able to survive without food during the heavy battle to come, asks for the chance to prove himself and later goes without food in preparation for battle, "refreshing" only by washing with water. The renewal phase of Guillaume and Rainouart is obvious here, but there is nonetheless also the constant reminder of work.

With the return to Orange and reminders of the fire and wasteland threatening the city, Guillaume is spurred on to preparation for the battle at Aliscans with the appropriate eating and drinking. Rainouart overindulges to the point that he would seem to be incapable of functioning as a warrior, and yet he is in the process of undergoing a transformation of one responsible for food as an apocalyptic image; the poet is beginning to sort out some contradictory images associated with him. Rainouart wishes to convert to another way of life separate from the kitchen, to "mature":

> Sire Guillames, je me vuel esprover.
> Trop longement m'ai laissié asoter.
> Si m'aïst diex! nel puis mais endurer.
> Ja en quisine ne quir mais converser,
> Se diex plaisoit, ains vaudroie amender.
> Mal soit dou fruit, ki ne veut meürer!
> Se le congié ne me volés doner,
> Par saint Denis, qui je doi aourer,
> Tous seus irai, qui k'en doie peser,
> En la bataille en Aliscans sor mer.
> (vv. 3356-65)

Rainouart is in the process of becoming a highly complex symbol representing both "food" and "conversion," and it is here that lies much of the uniqueness of this poem as compared with the *Chanson de Guillaume*. While, as in the latter, he again represents the food image, clearly responsible for providing the food so that work can be accomplished, he is also much more clearly responsible for the victory at Aliscans and for converting demonic elements into apocalyptic ones. But, Rainouart's conversion takes place over time. While he may continue to eat and drink to excess, he also provides the troops food and water when they must fight and prevents cowards from retreating to rest. As Rainouart is slowly

The Myth 25

converted into a proper knight, so does he "convert" *les couars* and *les faillis* as the great battle opens at Aliscans.

This Aliscans section is different from its counterpart in the *Chanson de Guillaume* in two ways: first, it contains the bean farmer episode which is absent from the earlier poem; and secondly, it demonstrates more clearly than the other that Rainouart can really trade places with Guillaume. It is Rainouart who becomes motivated by the polar apocalyptic and demonic images and who is responsible for defeating the Saracens more definitively than he does in the *Guillaume*.

The shift from Guillaume to Rainouart as the dominant figure in the Aliscans episode takes place over a period of some 1,500 lines. We learn early on that Rainouart is in charge of the recalcitrant Franks, but demonic imagery resumes immediately with reminders that the Saracens come from the sea and that Aliscans has been made a wasteland. Guillaume notes that he cannot rest, that he must work, but Rainouart soon takes over Guillaume's role in echoing these sentiments, finding himself confronted by Walegrape from the *mer betée*. Walegrape, it turns out, is Rainouart's brother, and this episode begins a pattern of reunions that will carry through to the end of the poem for Rainouart. He must battle Walegrape, Haucebier, and finally his cousin, Baudus. Of the three, only Baudus will ask for forgiveness and agree to be baptised, thereby evoking the apocalyptic water image that is followed by food in celebration. This is also followed by a rest phase for the Franks after a great deal of work. But interlaced with this narrative thread is the beginning of the bean farmer episode. All we know here is that a large contingent of Saracens has seized the bean field, a place that will serve as a food source as well as a place to pitch their tents. Once the celebration of Baudus's conversion has taken place, once he has departed for his homeland to bring back still more converts, and once the Franks have retired for the night, Rainouart rouses everyone well before daybreak. He first leads them out to visit the burial site of Vivien by the *estanc*, and then off on to adventure.

By chance they meet the bean farmer who tells them his tale of woe. He has seen the Saracens *toutes...essillier et gaster* (v. 7380). What should be a source of food has become a wasteland. The inverted image of the bean field spurs Rainouart on to a work phase again and he succeeds in eliminating all the Saracens, restoring to the farmer what beans are salvageable as well as awarding him the arms and horses of the offending pagans so that he will be able to provide bread for his children after all. Here ends the bean farmer episode and the great campaign at Aliscans.

The bean farmer episode might appear totally gratuitous were it not for the explanation that is to be offered by the archetypal structure of the Guillaume poems. Rainouart is not only responsible for providing food for the troops, but he is clearly also responsible for assuring that the land will conform to human proportions, that it will not remain in devastation, or that man's work to give it human proportions, to civilize it, will prevail. Rainouart takes upon himself a task normally assigned to Guillaume, a task that will reach its logical conclusion in the *Moniage Guillaume* as we will see shortly.

The final section of the *Aliscans* ties up the loose ends and witnesses the completion of the conversion process that Rainouart has been undergoing. As in the *Chanson de Guillaume*, the meal in celebration is marred by the Franks' slight of Rainouart. He swears to make a wasteland of Orange, specifically because he has been denied food. Upon his return and the revelation of his true identity, we witness his baptism, a meal, and the offer of rich clothing to this new member of the society. This presentation takes place under "two planted trees" (v. 7993). These trees, clearly not an accident of nature but consciously placed there by someone, represent not only nature and the rest phase of a cycle, but also the fact that man has here again given human proportions to nature. Nature serves man; the civilization goal is about to be reached. Rainouart's transformation is completed with his acquisition of new jousting skills, and Baudus returns with his men to strengthen the new society even further with their baptism. The final rest phase begins to be confirmed ultimately by Rainouart's marriage to Aelis, a symbol of the growth of the society on a microcosmic level and a symbol, although not strictly an archetypal one, of civilization or of building. This is particularly crucial for the *Aliscans*, for before a year is out Thibaut will ravage Orange and turn it into another wasteland. Then, when Guillaume bemoans his fate, Guibourc reminds him that life is one of change and regeneration, that

> Teus a perdu ki regaaignera,
> Et teus est povres qui riches devenra.
> Teus rit au main, au vespres ploërra.
> (vv. 8394-96)

Shortly afterward it is clearly sworn that one must *refai Orenge!* (v. 8413). The civilization goal has been reached with the strengthening and reaffirmation of the Frankish society, but we are never to forget the cyclical nature of life/death and work/rest: as Aelis dies giving birth to Maillefer, so we are also reminded that Guillaume's work is never done, that Rainouart, who has been given a fief, must be ever watchful of invasion from the sea bordering his lands. Guibourc's retelling of the Flood myth with its attendant motifs of destruction and rebuilding could not have been a more fitting conclusion to this epic poem with its emphasis upon devastation from the sea and man's response to it. Guillaume rebuilds his world in his own image and on his own terms. What demonic symbols from the sea he cannot make a part of his world are eliminated in blood and chased back into the sea to be "dissolved" by it; those he can integrate into his world are converted into apocalyptic ones through the regenerative waters of baptism. But the singular beauty of this lies in the fact that Rainouart takes on this regeneration and conversion as he himself shifts from the demonic to the apocalyptic, and at the same time guarantees the security of the kingdom and the civilization goal of Guillaume through an intricate dependancy upon the image of food.

By far the shortest poems in the Guillaume group, the *Charroi de Nîmes* and the *Prise d'Orange* may be considered together not only because of their brevity but also because of their close relationship to one another, the latter appearing very much as a sequel to the former. The four-level structure is less apparent in these two poems, the familiar apocalyptic and demonic images appearing more infrequently. This may be accounted for by the relative brevity of the poems, but the overall structure is the same, and it is still present even if in diminished quantity.

As expected, the opening of the *Charroi* builds up apocalyptic images and establishes that Guillaume is in a rest phase. The significant action begins when Bertran informs Guillaume that Louis is handing out lands to worthy knights. Guillaume is justifiably offended when he is overlooked. Louis offers him the lands and wife of the next lord to die, but this is unacceptable to Guillaume who makes it clear in subsequent discussions that he has no right to lands to which there may be a legal inheritor. The text reads in such a way that it is less a question of Guillaume's fear of possible reprisals by these inheritors and more a question of the fact that the maintenance of such lands is already assured. Neither can Guillaume accept one quarter of Louis's holdings as offered, for to do so would be to divide the kingdom. By asking rather for Spain, Tortelouse, Porpaillart, Nîmes, and Orange, he satisfies his own requirements: he does not weaken the kingdom, he does not intrude where the question of maintenance has already been satisfied, and he can build and increase the kingdom through his own work. Besides, Otrant has made a wasteland of Nîmes. Guillaume will increase Louis's honor—and obviously his kingdom—with iron and steel. Clearly Guillaume follows the pattern we have seen before, but this is reinforced all the more with reference to the important images as he recounts all he did for Louis in the *Couronnement* as well as the story of the devastation at Chartres.

The preparations for and the journey to Nîmes contain the usual apocalyptic images of food and nature, and in a somewhat ironic twist it is a foodstuff, represented by the barrel of salt, that gives rise to the *charroi* ruse. Once inside the city, insults, threats of fire, and the loss of two oxen to Saracen dinner tables are all that are needed to bring forth the battle. The barrels empty themselves of "iron and steel," and the city is liberated. As in the *Aliscans*, a food image, the salt barrel, becomes an underlying factor of the Franks' well-being. The usual food and drink in celebration restore the maintenance motif at the conclusion.

The *Prise* opens on the contraries suggested by the wasteland of Orange and the building motif represented by Orable who, once converted, will establish abbeys and monasteries. The narrative proper focuses on references to woods, fields, and water, as well as on Guillaume's attendance at Mass. The kingdom is at peace; Guillaume is in a rest phase. Enemies arrive from across the sea, however, and Guillaume affirms that *Que trop m'enuist ici a sejorner* (v. 67). This peaceful locus and all the accoutrements of civilization will be left behind once the messenger, Gillebert, appears from the water to tell of the trouble at Orange. He eats and drinks, but Guillaume fasts and even forgoes Mass until he has obtained Orable. She is obviously to be prized, but she also represents the potential conversion/completion syndrome necessary in re-establishing the maintenance motif.

Guillaume enters the demonic side of this epic world in crossing the Rhône and even disguising himself, pretending to be *d'outre mer*. He will nonetheless have to listen to threats expressed in terms of demonic images as well as be "unmasked" by Salatré, who appears from across the water. Ultimately, however, the demonic water motif becomes apocalyptic for the Franks as Guillebert escapes across the Rhône to Nîmes and returns with

Bertran and an army. With the liberation, Orable is baptised and married to Guilluame in a converted mosque. This is followed with the usual meal. The demonic world which Guillaume fearlessly entered has been completely turned into an apocalyptic one and brought to completion with the return of those elements of civilization upon which this poem had opened: harpers, jugglers, and rich clothing.

The *Moniage Guillaume* is the logical conclusion to the whole of this six-poem cycle and contains the keystone or final statement affirming the archetypal civilizing notion seen in the other poems. In leaving the *Charroi/Prise* and reaching the *Moniage,* the frequency and impact of the five archetypal images return. The Aniane section is built primarily upon the food image with heavy emphasis upon how much Guillaume eats and drinks as well as what a threat he poses to the order because of it. The monks had naturally offered him food and water upon his arrival, but it is obvious that the food image, as it is associated with Guillaume, promises to make a wasteland of the monastery. The demonic water image recurs as the monks wish that Guillaume would disappear across the *Rouge Mer* and hope that he may be drowned in the sea on the fish-buying expedition. But, Guillaume is as yet still in a rest phase, enjoying food and drink and hearing Mass in the morning before setting out.

The work phase begins as he enters the wasteland image, the Val de Sigré. The heavy irony of the *Moniage* then begins as Guillaume not only tricks the robbers into a fight upon his return through the Val with the fish, but also returns to Aniane with the robbers' goods with which he intends to decorate and enrich the monastery. Guillaume's work phase has been intended, albeit naively, to maintain the monastery. All this is reversed when he discovers how traitorous the monks have really been, and he slays the prior in a fit of anger. As atonement for his sins, and because he must obviously have a place of his own, he sets off into the *bois ramé* to establish his hermitage. The real work associated with the maintenance motif then comes to the fore.

Guillaume enters *terre pesme*, wandering through woods and hills, eating only what he stumbles across, and comes upon a hermit's hut in a pleasant valley by a river. Presumably he has just gone through an integrative phase and is entering a period of rest. But he is needed to stop the robbers from laying waste to the hermit's property. He takes food and rest, sleeps on grass and leaves, and finally does battle with the robbers with the usual victorious results. With the robbers gone they can now both work and sleep in security. But here, the notion of work takes on a different meaning than it has in the past for Guillaume. He has already declared he will leave his former life, the life of a knight; he is now more clearly concerned with the work of building a life out of the *desert* for himself.

Again he goes off through the woods. He finds not some ideal spot, but rather a stream, a fearsome place inhabited by serpents. He drowns them and enters another rest phase. It then becomes clearer to Guillaume what his true mission is: he walks over all the surrounding lands as if to make them his, tearing his clothes and injuring his hands on the rough surroundings, and going without food and drink this night, becoming one with his environment. He is renewed through a vision in which an angel tells him he will have even more work to do. This new type of work and the notion of renewal now becomes closely associated with one another. In true archetypal fashion he builds a hermitage out of the materials around him including a hut, a garden, and a chapel. Moreover, he makes his bed of the natural world which is the source of his food as well. He has become one with his world having lent it his own proportions. He also clears the land of the threat of a giant, throwing the beast into the water of a nearby stream, emphasizing that he is master of this world. Presumably the poem could end here except that Guillaume must still undergo more of this process and guarantee one final time the maintenance of the kingdom despite his vows to care only for the life of a monastic. Up to this point he has played nothing of his usual knightly role.

The Synagon episode offers him that opportunity. In his garden in order to *s'esbanoir*, Guillaume's rest phase ends as the Saracens threaten him with fire or drowning. He is taken prisoner and cast into an abominable *chartre* with a stream that rises with the tide, nearly drowning him, and where he must again compete with serpents. It is not until seven years later that new hope is born in the person of Landri who emerges from the sea, goes off to Paris to return with Louis and an army, and who then helps to liberate Guillaume. This is partially achieved by the Franks laying waste to the land around Palermo and forcing the Saracens to exhaust their food supply in the city. Guillaume then returns to his hermitage.

The Ysoré episode grows out of this pagan's anger at the Franks for having laid waste to Palermo. He threatens to do the same to the Franks, and in fact the wasteland and fire images are again evoked as they approach Paris. Louis's land does become a wasteland, and Anseis is sent to solicit help from Guillaume. During the visit in which Guillaume refuses to reveal his identity to Anseis, they enter the garden which the monk destroys and sows with thorns. As Ysoré threatens to destroy Paris, one symbol of civilization, Guillaume destroys the garden, a like symbol representing the successful integrative process of giving human proportions to nature.[7] Guillaume's microcosmic civilization in the desert will not be secure until the larger sphere is also.

When Guillaume arrives at the city he is unrecognized and rebuffed. With no place to stay he must go off *les un gaste cemin* seeking shelter in the hovel of Bertran del Fossé. Guillaume will once again turn the wasteland around the city into something acceptable, but he will also cleverly announce this with regard to Bertran's hut on the *gaste cemin*. Simply put, the hut is too small for Guillaume, but he "enlarges" it to fit his proportions. He then sends Bertran into the city for food so that they may refresh for the next day's work, and this suggests, as the very figure of Guillaume has always suggested, that the strength for victory really comes from within—it is a matter of knowing how to use it. The Saracens are defeated, "dissolved" in the Seine. There is food and drink in celebration, but Guillaume has returned to the hermitage without having identified himself, leaving it to Bertran to reveal the identity of the city's liberator when a false claimant to that honor would present himself. Even in his absence, Guillaume ensures that evil forces will not tear down the newly stabilized kingdom, the maintenance motif having once again been established. When he returns to his hermitage, Guillaume rebuilds his hut and replants his garden before his new rest period begins, a period based upon nature, food, and water images suggested by the location of the hermitage, the garden, and a nearby stream.

He enters one final and curious work period. A devil destroys a bridge the hero has built over the river, and for the next month Guillaume will rebuild the bridge by day only to have the devil destroy it by night.[8] The bridge is another symbol of civilization, Guillaume's attempt to reduce nature, or the river, to his own proportions. The devil is another wasteland symbol against which the hero has had to struggle all his life. Guillaume finally lies in wait for the devil one night, struggles with him and defeats him, throwing him into the river where a whirlpool will forever mark the spot. He then lives out his days in peace at the hermitage and finally enters Heaven.

The hero has spent his life fighting demonic symbols of human forces—Saracens. He has more recently struggled with nature to carve his own world out of the desert of Provence, an environment essentially hostile to man. He now struggles with the devil himself, a hostile supernatural force. Moreover, the whirlpool, which can now be safely traversed by Guillaume's bridge, is a final expression of man's ability to give human proportions to nature. The *Moniage* poet has understood full well the civilizing notion expressed throughout these poems of the Cycle, now giving Guillaume, in the twilight of his life, the chance to tame his most powerful adversary yet. Guillaume triumphs over the devil, good triumphs over evil, man triumphs over nature. Here, the devil is perhaps the medieval epic poet's only metaphor for the most powerful forces in the world of this poetry. It would be *invraisemblable* for Guillaume to engage true natural forces such as tornadoes or hurricanes, but the poet can suggest such forces with the metaphor of the devil, an image which the medieval listener will also interpret as "evil." Thus, this final episode in Guillaume's life prior to his eternal rest in Heaven allows several levels of interpretation. He has by now quite literally triumphed over the world of his desert, the flesh of the Saracens, and the devil of the bridge. Guillaume has finally ended his quest. He has civilized his world turning all demonic images into apocalyptic ones with which he can be comfortably integrated. The *Moniage* is a perfect example of "poetry (from an archetypal point of view) as part of the total human imitation of nature that we call civilization. Civilization...not merely (as) imitation of nature, but the process of making a total human form out of nature..." (Frye 105).

The description of the whirlpool at the end of the *Moniage* comes at the end of the next to the last laisse, and it is repeated for emphasis at the beginning of the last laisse:

> Ainc li diables puis ne s'en remua,
> Tous tans i gist et tous tans i girra.
> L'aighe i tournoie, ja coie ne sera,
> Grans est la fosse et noire contreval.
>
> Quant le diables fu en l'aighe parfont,
> L'aighe i tornoie entor et environ;

> Grans est la fosse, nus n'i puet prendre fons.
> Maint pelerin le voient qui la sont,
> Et saint Guillaume sovent requis i ont;
> Caillaus et pierres getent el puis parfont.
> (vv. 6611-20)

The whirlpool is in fact referred to in the text as a *fosse*; it is dark and bottomless, and it swallows up the stones pilgrims toss into it. The *fosse* here is the symbol of the foreboding wasteland Guillaume has struggled against throughout the six poems; it offers yet another dimension, along with that of the image of the devil transformed, to the suggestion that Guillaume has overcome negative forces. It is the final image of a long process over time where Guillaume has managed to convert a wasteland image into something manageable. This is a process carefully signaled by the *Moniage* poet in Guillaume's acceptance of Bertran's *fosse* as a base for his last act of ridding his world of the Saracen threat. Christ-like, the unrecognized, rebuffed hero unashamedly debases himself in order to perform his deliverance of the city (e.g., mankind), leaving it to another to reveal his identity to his fellow man in his absence. The *fosse*, the outer darkness, is thus ultimately rendered harmless, a bottomless pit where the faithful may fairly nonchalantly mock the negative force by casting into this void those stones which could as easily represent his building materials as they could the crumbled ruins of man's inventions. The civilization goal has finally been reached, the long dialectical process of maintenance and destruction having finally been transcended. The building stones are no longer needed, but so too can man cast into the bottomless pit the last vestiges of chaos or of his world destroyed. Guillaume cannot live forever, but he can leave behind a world transformed in his image: a shelter, a garden, a chapel, and the harmless void of the whirlpool. In these epics the city as archetypal image is of less concern than its microcosmic counterpart, the house. Guillaume does not need to found a city, for his concerns are of a more individual nature. In any case, the mineral, vegetable, and dual spiritual expressions of Guillaume's consciousness will remain. The animus, the efficient cause of man's *gestes* in this world, is finally free to leave. The "petit cycle" of Guillaume is complete.

Chapter Three
Semiosis of the Myth

WE HAVE RELIED UPON A POLAR STRUCTURE of opposing images and motifs in order to understand the basis for the civilization myth in the Guillaume Cycle. It is, in fact, a series of opposing forces or states which generate the action of the poem and advance the narrative with expressions of one pole responding to the momentary dominance of the other. In this chapter we turn to a discussion of just how the myth is communicated to a listening audience through this polar structure, that is to the semiosis of the myth.

Questions of polarity and myth are necessary points of departure for a study of the semiosis of the Guillaume poems, for semiosis itself presumes contrast or opposition. Simply stated, meaning and evaluation depend upon some minimal notion of differentiation. "Black" is therefore meaningless unless it is understood in terms of something else such as "white." Likewise with "tall/short," "beautiful/ugly," and so forth. Thus in regard to the Guillaume poems, "fire" really carries no clear signification until it comes to be understood in contrast to "water." The same applies to the apocalyptic water image in contrast to its demonic counterpart. In fact, nothing in these poems really takes on any value until it is held to be in some sort of opposition or correlation to something else.[1] This characteristic applies not only to specific images, but extends also to the maintenance and destruction motifs as well as to Guillaume's states of work and rest. Each element of these pairs is defined within the text in relation to the other element, but the subsequent and crucial result of this opposition is that this binary relationship is ultimately to be overcome or resolved and drawn into a unity. Such is the stuff of myth.

In order to function, the binary principle must bring about some movement in the narrative, and it is precisely because of contrast or opposition that action takes place. As we have already seen, Guillaume responds to certain demonic images because he evaluates them in certain ways. Evaluation, therefore, is preliminary to action, or we might suggest the following as a pattern for narrative development in these epics:

opposition → evaluation → response

where opposition is also understood as disjunction or nonconjunction. Thus it is that simple disjunction of binary pairs is the basis for meaning and movement within the text.

Numerous studies have appeared in recent years which have attempted to describe from one point of view or another the process of narration. The works of Barthes ("An Introduction to the Structural Analysis of Narrative"), Bremond (*La logique du récit*), Greimas (*Sémantique structurale*), Todorov (*Grammaire du Décameron*, "Les catégories du récit littéraire"), and Kristeva (*La texte du roman*) come immediately to mind. Our own theory of the semiosis of the myth of Guillaume in this Cycle is informed in large measure by Barthes, Greimas, and Kristeva, as well as Eco (*A Theory of Semiotics*) whose ideas on the generation of the sememe are particularly useful.

As with any narrative, the Guillaume poems are composed of both syntagmatic and paradigmatic elements. These two axes allow the poetic space of the poems to develop, and they encompass both the static and dynamic aspects of the narrative. These axes are also dependant upon one another; it is difficult to imagine a literary work in which only one could exist without the other. To suggest that there might only be a syntagmatic aspect would be to allow for movement, or action, but would be to disallow any consistency of character, any referential aspect between situations or functions, any use of symbol or metaphor. An example of such a structure would presumably be an isolated syntagm, perhaps one sentence. Such would hardly be a narrative text in the sense in which we usually think of it. Likewise, we could really have no narrative at all with a text consisting only of a paradigmatic feature. Such a text might have characters and situations as well as symbols and metaphors, but there would be no action or movement, nothing in the way of metonymy, nothing suggesting contiguity, consequence, or sequence of any kind.

All literature is not structured alike, however, with respect to syntagmatic and paradigmatic aspects, and Old French epics of the Guillaume Cycle are unique in that they exhibit a greater dependancy upon the paradigmatic than the syntagmatic element. This is not surprising considering their mythic, archetypal nature. As Lévi-Strauss has shown again and again, the stable form of a myth throughout all its variants is one of the laws of mythic transformation (e.g., *Mythologiques*). Now while he is talking about primitive myths, not medieval epics, and about variant texts, not one single text, the principle is applicable and worth nothing here: mythical thought relies upon a paradigmatic association of ideas, events, and particularly symbols and archetypes. The Guillaume poems, as we saw earlier, rely upon a constant and limited semanticization of particular images, or what Kristeva would call "unités de restriction," an idea to which we shall return later. It is in the paradigmatic aspect that this symbolization and its restriction takes place, and thus we find a heavy dependency upon it in these epics.

The syntagmatic aspect is just as essential even if it is not as critical to the formation of the mythic framework of the poem. There must be narration, movement. In fact, without the syntagmatic aspect there would be no development of verticality, of the associative function, of symbols and archetypes. These elements can only be developed or semanticized over the time of the narration and through the process of narration. "Fire" becomes significant only through repetitive and restrictive use. If in a given poem it is immediately recognized in its restrictive uniqueness the first time it appears, it is only because that semanticization has already been developed in another poem which itself is then "slotted" paradigmatically as a mythic image, the various elements of which (i.e., images, archetypes, symbols) stand in an associative relationship to subsequent elements in subsequent poems. Here, however, we are getting into the area of mythic images to which we shall have to return later.

The composition of the syntagmatic aspect of the Guillaume poems is perhaps the easiest place to begin examination of their semiosis simply because it is the horizontality of the narrative we recognize first. Here we may divide this aspect into the two large Platonic categories of mimesis and diegesis, the former relating to direct discourse, the latter to what we recognize as authorial narration.[2]

Diegesis serves as the basic framework for the syntagmatic relations. Gerard Genette divides it into the two aspects of narration and description, the latter being the more indispensable; it is entirely possible, he reasons, to have a text composed primarily or solely of narration ("Frontières du récit"). This division into narration and description is not only a logical one, but it is certainly applicable to epic literature. Genette then further divides description into the decor and explicative/symbolic functions, decor suggesting simple description of settings and situations without "loading" them semantically, the explicative/symbolic function suggesting highly charged, or uniquely or archetypally semanticized images.

Still within the aspect of diegesis we then encounter situations bringing about change, that is to say movement or direction, in the narrative and the characters involved in these situations. These are areas which have been widely discussed, the first most notably associated with Vladimir Propp and his functional analyses (*Morphology of the Folktale*), the second with Greimas and the method of actantial analysis (*Sémantique structurale*). Propp's and Greimas's approaches to narrative may not necessarily be applicable to all literary genres; I do not find them particularly instructive for Old French epics.[3] In his proposal for an approach to narrative analysis in 1966, Roland Barthes ("An Introduction to the Structural Analysis of Narrative") suggested three structural levels: functions (cf. Propp and Bremond), actions (cf. Greimas), and narration (cf. Todorov). This was very useful and one of the most logical overall approaches to narrative analysis at the time, and it still holds merit today. It may not be particularly applicable to the epics, however, and in any case I am not sure that one can really say, as Barthes does, that functions are more elemental than actions. There really is no such thing as a function without an action. Let us say, rather, that instead of functions and actions, what we are really dealing with are smaller units of these respective categories, at least for the Guillaume epics. We will call them encounters and characters respectively.[4]

By encounters we understand situations which potentially cause a character to act or to react in a particular way. Again, it is impossible, perhaps more importantly unnecessary, to say which is more elemental, the encounter or the character. Presumably we can have an encounter in the absence of a character so long as the character sooner or later arrives on the scene and responds to the situation. Likewise it is possible to introduce a character into a descriptive setting with no occurrence of encounters. In any case, the crucial point is that neither characters nor encounters really take on any meaning in the total absence of the other as far as the larger text is concerned. Let us say, therefore, that these two elements of the diegesis must develop roughly simultaneously. It might be argued that in beginning *in medias res* one could totally by-pass any description in which to embed characters and an encounter, but even that is unlikely. Description does not have to take the form of some nineteenth-century realistic notion of decor and setting. We need have only the barest framework in which to set an encounter, and in every Old French epic I can think of, this is at least the case. In fact, it is most often the case in the typical "bare stage" technique of the epic.

Once we arrive at the level of encounters and characters, we pass then to the level of narration, the other half of Genette's division of diegesis (or the third level of Barthes's division of the overall narrative). In the Guillaume poems, it is here that those levels of decor and symbols, encounters and characters, come together in a first approximation of a flowing narrative, that is movement around or because of a particular situation involving specific characters and in a given setting. Such movement has vector-like qualities, that is both force and direction. The force is provided by either positive or negative response of one or more characters to an encounter; this force is thus the result of a static polar relationship, or, that is to say, movement comes about because of attraction or repulsion of two "poles" for one another. Another way of saying this is that disjunction is responsible for the *récit*. The direction is toward ultimate resolution of the conflict between, or unification of, the pair of oppositions. Obviously a given opposition may be resolved immediately, but this does not mean that the narrative then becomes stagnant or directionless. In the Guillaume epics as elsewhere, pairs of opposition are constantly being evoked anew or are never really resolved to begin with. The narrative thus continues with force and direction toward a goal which may or may not be evident early on in this process.

At such a level we are at the point where diegesis really becomes recognizable as such, but what we have seen so far does not provide the whole picture of narration. Two elements which also enter at this point and which help to control narration are iconic and indexical signs. They are responsible for retarding or even stopping the narrative flow momentarily. Iconic signs are complex images or tableaux which cause us to focus on a particular scene or the idea it represents as in stop-action. The magnificent death scene of Vivien in *Aliscans* or the *braies* episode of the *Moniage* are examples of iconic signs. Indexical signs have temporal rather than spatial functions. Such formulas as *biaus fu li jors, li solaus raia cler*, or *ne vos targies mie* either momentarily stop the narrative flow in the brief moments underlined or reduce long spans of time into a fraction of the time needed to effect an action such as riding from one locus to another. Iconic and indexical signs, about which more later, tend to stop or to interrupt the narrative flow in the syntagmatic element, and they are integral parts of the paradigmatic element of the text.

Mimesis then, the other half of the syntagmatic element, is really embedded in diegesis. Mimesis may contain all of the elements to be found in diegesis certainly, but, again, it is unlikely that one would ever encounter a sustained example of pure mimesis; it is certainly not to be found in Old French epics. In the epic text, mimesis is primarily for adornment and for heightening the dramatic tension of the text, and as such it properly belongs to the syntagmatic element as a reflection of, or as a function of, diegesis.

The paradigmatic, or vertical, aspect of the text consists of those elements which exist outside of the temporal flow of the narrative. Included here are semes, sememes, and the mythemes they generate, iconic and indexical signs, characters and encounters, and all those aspects of description necessary to create settings and tableaux such as their semes, sememes, and symbols. To the extent that these elements do exist outside of time, to the extent that they become formulaic, to the extent that they reflect back upon one another, and to the extent that they become fixed as repetitive formulas, functions, and images, they are pardigmatic.

The paradigmatic function of the epic text has two roles, the first of which is to stop the narrative flow momentarily, and the second of which, as a consequence of the first, is to expand an image vertically in order to give it the epic or mythic proportions which we associate with these poems. The paradigmatic elements of an epic text play a greater role than they might in something such as a novel of realism where the narrative flow or syntagmatic function would be stronger because of the importance of a sense of human time. In the epic text, it is essential that the flow be stopped periodically, even frequently, to allow for the mythic expansion of certain images, for it is only through the elevation of these images to such proportions that the didactic nature of the message of the text can be effected. If, as I affirm, an epic has as its purpose to provide a model for behavior or for a way of looking at the world, then it is indeed didactic, and one way of executing a didactic text is precisely that of the epic: a repetitive heightening of critical images of characters, scenes, encounters, and actions such that they become fixed extra-temporally in the listener's mind with no room for false interpretation of their intended messages.

Several things may now be said regarding the interaction of the syntagmatic and paradigmatic aspects of the epic text. These aspects are dependent upon one another. While it is the paradigmatic aspect which is responsible for the generation of mythemes and thus the message of the text, and while these mythemes are extra-temporal, they only become significant over time or through the syntagmatic flow of the narrative. The *récit* must progress for the paradigmatic elements to assume their associative relationships and to become semanticized. Likewise, there is no horizontal movement without the paradigmatic function, that is without the periodic recurrence of certain signs which cause action to develop. The syntagmatic and paradigmatic functions of the text are thus in constant opposition with, as well as dependent upon, one another, and this is reasonable to expect for just as the action itself is generated by disjunction and must depend upon it if there is to be any movement in the narrative, the larger structure of the text assumes these same relationships if it is to be structurally unified.

Still, however, we can find two basic kinds of narrative structure within the Guillaume epics, structures we call fluid and imagistic narratives. The first refers to that kind of narrative which moves along rather smoothly, relatively uninterrupted by dominant paradigmatic elements such as mythemes, archetypal sememes, iconic and indexical signs. The second is the inverse of the first, that is a narrative which appears to progress more or less by a series of tableaux or mythic images. The first type naturally is closer to what we would call realistic narrative with our notions of continuous space and chronology respected. Chronology and continuous space in the imagistic type may be anywhere from mildly to grossly distorted. Examples of fluid narrative would be passages such as those describing the scene at Laon when Guillaume must go to Louis to seek his aid in *Aliscans* and the scene at Paris in the Ysoré episode of the *Moniage*. The action in both of these examples is straightforward and about as "realistic" as epic action can be. In the *Chanson de Guillaume*, however, the Vivien passage tends to be imagistic with the camera-eye shifting from Vivien to the enemy, to the *duit troblé*, to memories of all that has been left behind in "sweet France," to the enemy ships *es haltes eigues*, and so on. [5]

It is clearly the poet who manipulates mimesis and diegesis in structuring the text, creating certain images and messages by focusing on particular aspects, and lending a certain tone and style to the work. If we may speak only of the text itself, however, the poem and its message are really dependent at base upon diegesis, and within diegesis they are dependent upon its descriptive function. It is here that things begin to move and that semanticization takes place due to the principle of opposition and that narration and even mimesis can follow. When we then finally reach the level of narration as such, it is there where stylistic aspects such as irony, comedy, and seriousness, that is tone and mode, become evident. They are dependant upon the proper semanticization of images in lower levels of diegesis and mimesis.

We have said nothing yet about several other important elements of the epic text, that is time, space, and intertextuality. These elements properly belong to the paradigmatic function of the text and operate, as with iconic and indexical signs, to interrupt narrative flow or to assist in mythifying the work. Intertextuality will be taken up at the end of this chapter, time and space in subsequent chapters.

We have described the narrative macrostructure of the epic text as being built up horizontally of successive levels of description (decor and explicative/symbolic functions), characters and encounters, and finally movement with as yet undetermined rules of action entering at the level of characters and encounters. On the vertical plane of the text are those elements which tend to mythify it or to retard and interrupt the narrative, such as mythemes, iconic and indexical signs, and so forth. This narrative structure with its horizontal and vertical planes now really renders the four-level structure discussed in the previous chapter inadequate. The latter was useful for picturing the archetypal nature of the myth from the point of view of Guillaume's behavior, but a detailed analysis of the narrative as just described here will enable us to arrive at an understanding of the semiosis of the myth. Before attempting that, however, let us see what relationship the four-level archetypal structure may have to the horizontal and vertical axes of the narrative.

The five images of level I of Figure I are part of the descriptive level of the narrative and properly belong to the explicative/symbolic sublevel. They are more than just decor; they possess a very specific function and meaning, for they ultimately comprise part of the "encounter" level and will, in combination with specific characters, cause the vectored movement of the narrative. In Figure I we saw them generate maintenance and destruction motifs. These are also aspects of our "encounter" level, for in fact it is more correctly these motifs to which Guillaume will respond, that is the connotations of *fire, water, wasteland*, etc., not simply the images themselves. As simple images (decor), they are almost meaningless, or at least inconsequential with respect to narrative development. When they become semanticized in particular ways, however, it is their symbolic functions which come into play. The work/rest cycle then belongs to the movement level of the narrative macrostructure. The civilization goal, however, cannot be assigned to the syntagmatic aspect of the text; it is paradigmatic, existing totally outside of the time of the text. It is that vertical component toward which Guillaume works throughout but which itself never really enters the narrative. However, none of this is still sufficient to understand the semiosis of the myth for we have not gotten down to those smallest elements which inform the message of the text by virtue of the principle of opposition.

According to a strict structuralist approach to this analysis we should begin at the level of phonemes as the smallest units of differentiation in a text. This is not only unnecessary for our purposes, but it would also provide for needless complications in that phonemically it will be impossible to draw the lines of opposition between pairs such as "maintenance/destruction," "work/rest," or apocalyptic *eau*/demonic *eau*.[6] If we cannot start at the phonemic level, we can, however, with no loss to either interpretation of the message of the text or to verifiability, begin on the semantic level. Thus we focus on that minimal unit of meaning, the seme.

There are various possible approaches to the semiology of these texts, the best of which might be suggested by Greimas (*Sémantique structurale*) and Eco (*A Theory of Semiotics*). Eco's approach will be the most helpful, although some of what follows has been influenced by Greimas as well. Let us start with the following model:

Figure II

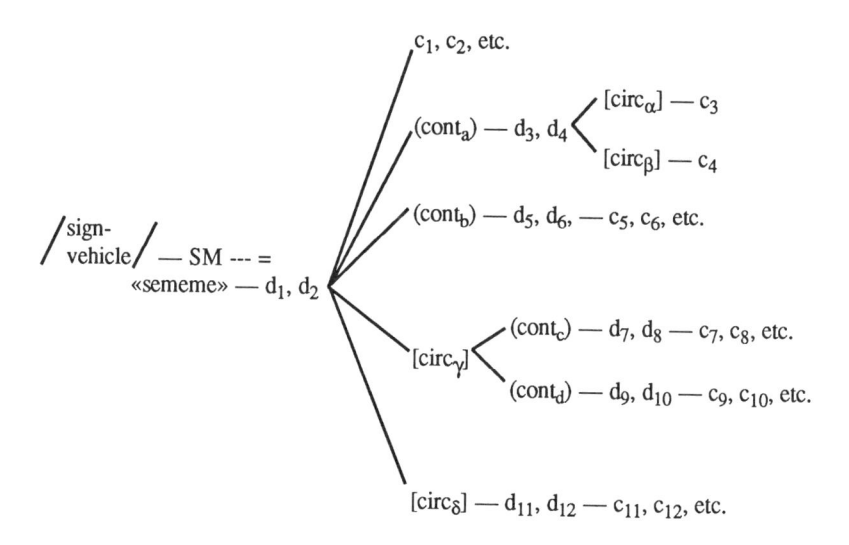

```
                                    c₁, c₂, etc.
                                   /
                                  /         [circ_α] — c₃
                          (cont_a) — d₃, d₄ <
                         /                   [circ_β] — c₄
                        /
 /sign-  /              / (cont_b) — d₅, d₆, — c₅, c₆, etc.
/vehicle/ — SM --- = <
          «sememe» — d₁, d₂
                        \              (cont_c) — d₇, d₈ — c₇, c₈, etc.
                         \    [circ_γ] <
                          \            (cont_d) — d₉, d₁₀ — c₉, c₁₀, etc.
                           \
                            [circ_δ] — d₁₁, d₁₂ — c₁₁, c₁₂, etc.
```

/sv/ is the sign vehicle of a sememe or content unit, <s>, say <water>. The sign vehicle is that graphic convention of the text, that is the word or lexeme, /water/. Behind it, as shown in the model, lies the sememe which itself is made up of a cluster of semes which Eco calls denotata, "d," and connotata, "c," (84-120) and which Greimas would call properties of object-terms (27-54). These might loosely be called qualities, although as will be seen in the following discussion, that is really not a very adequate term. As the model shows, it is not sufficient to describe a sememe or content unit as composed simply of a cluster of semes even though there would be no fixed number of semes for a given sememe. We must also determine the context, "CONT," and circumstance, "CIRC," in which a sememe occurs if we are to understand it properly. Theoretically it is possible for either a CONT or CIRC to embed the other, but that will not be a critical factor in our discussion.

Let us look at an example from the Guillaume epics. <Water>, as we know, can occur in the two contexts of "maintenance" and "destruction." In the context of "maintenance," it is found primarily in these circumstances: "baptism," "drink," or "washing." Each of these circumstances is then in turn defined by specific semes which occur in two modes, the denotative and connotative. It is at this level that the variety and richness of a sememe is found; it is also here that much of the tone and mode (e.g., irony, comedy) of the text are generated as well as misunderstanding and misinterpretation of it. If the connotations in particular are not read out carefully, there will be confusion or even "blindness" on the part of the receiver of the message.

In the circumstance of baptism we would find denotata such as "acceptance of the faith" and "membership in the Church," with connotata such as "unity with God," "everlasting life," "spiritual refreshment." The circumstance of drink would denote "refreshment" and "slaking of thirst" and connote "well-being" as well as "rest from labors." And the circumstance of washing would denote "cleansing" while connoting "refreshment," "well-being," and "rest from labors." As can be seen here, what are denotata in some circumstances can be connotata in others, and we would expect to find the inverse to be true as well.

As for the context of destruction, we have generally found <water> to occur in a circumstance of "drowning." This denotes "death" and "dissolution" while connoting "elimination from the society," "failure in one's mission," and "victory for the enemy." Obviously, we have not identified all the possible denotata and connotata possible for the various circumstances and contexts of (water) in the Guillaume poems, but the foregoing is sufficient to demonstrate the complexity and the composition of such a sememe in these texts. What we must note, however, is that the principle of opposition is operative everywhere in the model just presented.

With regard to our five archetypal images there are always apocalyptic and demonic contexts with the exception of "wasteland." Even in such a case, however, there is the inherent polarity with an undemonstrated positive aspect to this image. "Wasteland" is a meaningless term unless it is understood in terms of something such as an archetypal garden image or even, perhaps, an image of "wasteland" suggesting not devastation and ruin but rather the potential for growth and development.

The point is that both poles of the comparison need not be present in the text for an image to have any meaning.

The principle of opposition is not, however, carried over into the various circumstances embedded within their respective contexts; that is, there will not be two possible circumstances for every context. The opposition in terms of circumstances is reflected between positive and negative contexts (maintenance/destruction), or, in other words, the opposite of a circumstance will be found not in the same context but in a contrasting one. This is also true for all of the semes, the denotata, and connotata. But with regard to circumstances and semes, we must realize that they are again meaningless terms unless understood in terms of their opposites. "Unity with God" is meaningful only insofar as we also recognize the possibility of "separation from God."

This demonstration with <water> shows the possibilities of the semantic model proposed by Eco, but it by no means satisfies all the possibilities of our texts. The total collection of sememes can be divided into animate and inanimate categories the longer of which is the latter and which also includes the five archetypal images with which we have dealt. The animate sememes, that is horses, oxen, and the like are not necessarily different from nonarchetypal inanimate ones in terms of importance or composition, but the animate-human sememes—characters—can be quite complex. Let us look at a few examples.

The nonarchetypal inanimate sememes are the simplest of all because they are not highly charged symbols. They are merely used as tools which are quickly discarded once they have served their purpose; they usually do not take on the number of semes that archetypal sememes do. An example such as the palace tower of the *Prise d'Orange* will demonstrate this.

The palace is found in a context of enemy territory into which are embedded two circumstances: "Guillaume as un unrecognized Frankish intruder," and "Guillaume as a captive." In the first circumstance the denotata are "Saracen," "Orable," "enemy," "headquarters," "officers," "royalty," "foreign tongue"; the connotata are "potential danger," "love," "wealth," "separation from Frankish forces," "necessity for disguise," "opportunity for Frankish expansion." In the circumstances of Guillaume's captivity the denotata are "Saracen," "enemy," "headquarters," "officers," " royalty," "Orable," "foreign tongue," " entrapment," "imminent danger"; the connotata are then "death," "separation from Frankish forces," "identity revealed," "no opportunity for Frankish expansion," "failure of mission," "supremacy of Saracens."

An example of a sememe which would be even less complicated than the palace at Orange might be Gaidon's hut in the desert of Provence in the *Moniage*. Here we find a context of "wilderness hermitage" and a circumstance of "attack by a giant." The denotata are "holy man," "solitude," "danger," "poverty," while the connotata are "destruction," "potential death," "disruption of monastic life."

The sememes <palace at Orange> and <Gaidon's hut> compose part of the decor element of the diegesis in their respective poems and as such they do not enter significantly into the symbolic content of their texts. The situation is considerably different for an inanimate sememe such as Rainouart's *tinel* or the bean field found in the *Aliscans*, for both of these contribute directly to the symbolic function of description. The *tinel* is found in the two contexts of "defense" and "aggression," and within the "aggression" context there are the two circumstances of "towards the Saracens" and "toward the Franks"; the circumstance of "against the Franks" occurs in the "defense" context. In the latter we find the denotata "belonging to Saracen," "defensive weapon," "wooden," "heavy" and the connotata of "death," "injury," "pain," "low-class," "unrefined," "self-protection." In an "aggressive" context of circumstance "toward the Saracens" we find the denotata of "belonging to Saracen," "aggressive weapon," "wooden," "heavy" and the connotata "death," "injury," "pain," "low-class," "unrefined," "victory over Saracens/countrymen," "victory for Franks," "expansion of Frankish realm." In the "aggressive" context of circumstance "toward the Franks" (such as at the end of the *Chanson de Guillaume* where he must be persuaded to return to the palace) we find the same denotata as in the other "aggressive" context, but the connotata are "death," "injury," "pain," "low-class," "unrefined," "threat of victory for Saracens," "threat of defeat for Franks," "threat of sudden reduction of Frankish realm." Thus the sememe *tinel* takes on a wide range of semes, and like the archetypal images it does so over time. We can, therefore, isolate a particular contextually, circumstantially defined image of *tinel* and describe its semic properties, but we can only describe its total or mythic image once we have experienced all the possible occurrences of this important image. Again, we will defer discussion of mythic images until later, but suffice it to say here that *tinel* becomes highly symbolic, representing ultimate victory for the Franks at the hands of one of their enemy's own. That is to say, *tinel* symbolizes victorious reversal.

The sememe <bean field> also has a highly symbolic function. In its one occurrence, in the *Aliscans*, the circumstance of which is "plundering Saracens," we discover the following denotata: "peasant," "farm," "food"; the connotata are "well-being," "growth," "happiness," "health," "peace of mind," "familial unity." Symbolically this image becomes synonymous with the civilization image toward which Guillaume and, in this case, Rainouart are working. Thus, when it becomes threatened, the threat will generate the same kind of response from Rainouart that we find coming from Guillaume when he is confronted by demonic fire or water images.

The question now arises as to the difference between inanimate sememes belonging to the decor function and those belonging to the symbolic function of diegesis. The answer, as suggested by the foregoing discussion, is that decor sememes do not relate directly to any other level of the narrative structure. Conversely, symbolic sememes relate directly to the level of encounters where they become integral parts of the encounter situation and subsequently bring about movement in the narrative because of a character's response to the situation with which he is confronted.

This brings us to the question of the animate sememes of which there are two types, human and nonhuman. The latter refer naturally to such things as horses; we will assume that ferocious giants are "human" although there may be some room for some debate on this point. The nonhuman animate sememes are fairly simple, because, again, they do not directly relate to the encounter level except as part of decor. *Destrier*, for example, is found in the context of battle with denotata of "animate," "nonhuman," "four-legged," "domesticated," "large," "capable of carriage," "powerful," and connotata of "fearlessness," "obedience," "help to knight," "possible injury or death to adversary," "potential victory for knight."[7] Such a sememe really becomes a stock formula in the epic, changing little if at all from one circumstance to another. If, however, a particular *destrier* is given a specific identity (e.g., "Baucent"), then it takes on additional semes such as "fidelity," "friendship," and so on, but this still does not alter the basic sememe appreciably with respect to the overall myth.

Human sememes are another thing. Obviously they will relate to the encounter level where the action of the poem is put into play, but they are still more complex in that they are constantly in the process of accreting meaning because of the possible addition of semes in new contexts or circumstances. Let us look first at the sememe <Guillaume>.

It is difficult to outline the "basic" sememe of this character, for the larger mythic image of him that we know through having encountered his various aspects in the Cycle colors our view of him. The following is, therefore, an approximation. As a hypothetical case let us take Guillaume in the context of "defense of land or property" and in the circumstance of "against the traitor Arneis" (*Couronnement*). Here we find denotata of "animate," "human," "Frankish," "large," "knight," "defender of Crown," and the connotata "fearsome," "fearless," "tireless," "strong," "brave," "one-minded," "victory for Franks and Crown," "protector of Peace." These semes should be found in any context and circumstance of an occurrence of the image of Guillaume. In the situation we mention here, however, we could also add the connotata of "defender of widows and orphans" which he picks up from Charles's instructions to Louis, "hateful toward traitors" because of his disdainful attitude toward Arneis, "perfect loyalty" because of his failure to try to seize power for himself, and "desire to increase Frankish influence" because of his pilgrimage to Rome at this time. We would then find still other semes added to the basic sememe <Guillaume> in other contexts and circumstances: "defender of the weak" (Bertran and Gaidon in the *Moniage*), "clever" (Val de Sigre episode of the *Moniage*, barrel ruse of the *Charroi*), "bluntly honest" (Laon episode with Blancheflor in the *Guillaume*), "thoughtless" (omission of Rainouart from the last dinner in *Guillaume* and *Aliscans*), and so on. The list could be extended considerably.

Each of the additional semes we have identified as coming from unique contexts and circumstances are connotata, not denotata. This may be obvious, but what is important is that for a given character there will probably be a fixed number of denotata, while there will be a potentially limitless number of connotata. Thus it is the connotative semes which offer the richness, variety, and depth that can be found in these characters, and any major character can and will be constructed semically in the same way that <Guillaume> is. Rainouart, for example, who is much easier to draw since he appears much less often, would be defined by the context "former Saracen" in the circumstance "kitchen knave at Louis's court," by the denotata "animate," "large," "*tinel*," "human," "Saracen," "cook," "scruffy," "ill-tempered" and the connotata "defensive," "poor," "low-class," "violent," "dangerous," "strong," "undisciplined," "unorthodox warrior," "hateful." In other circumstances, then, we would find such additional semes as "defense of Frankish interests" (battle at Archamps in *Guillaume* and *Aliscans*), "loyalty to Franks against former countrymen" (Archamps in *Guillaume* and *Aliscans*), "potential destroyer of Frankish peace" (final dinner scene in *Guillaume* and *Aliscans*), and "archetypal civilizer" (bean field episode of *Aliscans*).

But we are really not through with <Guillaume>, for as we have just described him he is semically no different from Rainouart, nor would he be different structurally from any other major character (e.g., Guibourc), even though he would be composed of different semes. Guillaume is the one character, however, who will respond to our five archetypal images. Thus we find that over time <Guillaume> connotes "anger at the demonic images" and "pleasure at apocalyptic images." The result of this is his cyclical response at the level of encounters. It is certainly true that other characters will respond at the level of encounters to certain stimuli and will thus be prodded into action, but the difference between Guillaume and all other characters is that his response comes directly and consistently from archetypal symbols on the descriptive level, not from ordinary threats or the mere presence of an enemy. We find again, then, that the five images relate directly to the encounter level of the narrative, operating in a vertical fashion.

So far we have described the composition of animate and inanimate sememes, that is the decor, symbolic, and character functions of the text, and we have noted that the archetypal sememes and characters relate directly to the encounter level. Again, we remind ourselves that everything up to this point is based upon the principle of opposition, even the simplest of inanimate sememes (eg. demonic <fire> denotes "hot/cold" and connotes "death/life," and so on). This principle is also operative at the encounter level in two ways.

First, there can be no movement in the text unless some kind of opposition arises which overbalances a prevailing directional force or disrupts a static situation. An example of the overbalancing of one force by another would be the arrival of Rainouart in the *Guillaume* or in the *Aliscans* at the moment when things are not going well for the Franks followed by the subsequent turn of events. An example of the disruption of the status quo is found at the beginning of the *Charroi* where all seems at peace. It is May, the birds and fields are awakening, and Guillaume is returning from his *locus amoenus* when confronted by Bertran with the news that others have been rewarded for their service to the Crown, but that he has been overlooked.

Second, the rules of action which dictate the kind of response to a given situation are the result of an opposition in that they are meaningless unless understood in light of their potential opposites. To put it another way, action results because there is but one choice. Yet in the epic world there is but one choice because its inverse is totally unacceptable. Rainouart cannot refuse to help Guillaume because he has by now become imbued with a certain loyalty to the Franks. Guillaume cannot respond at the opening of the *Charroi* in any way other than he does because to do so would be to contradict his character. Thus, he must seek out his own reward because not to do so would be to render him *lache* or *fainéant*, neither of which fit him semically. He must seek his reward in lands not yet belonging to the Franks. If he were to take any lands Louis has to offer, the result would be to split the kingdom or to redouble unnecessarily the maintenance efforts of lands already endowed with descendants to look after them. Neither of these lines of action would fit him semically either; we already know (*Couronnement*) that he wants to *creiste ses terres*, his and the Crown's.

The movement which grows out of the encounter level is the result of three factors coming together simultaneously: (1) characters, (2) situations, and (3) rules of action. The characters and situations are obviously semically defined; the rules of action operate as "natural laws" within the epic genre offering direction but remaining exterior to the narrative flow itself. This level of the text would involve what Propp would call functions and what Greimas would call actants. That is, it would be composed of categories of situations such as "arrival," "departure," "misdeed," "lack," and classes of forces such as "sender," "receiver," "adjuvant," "opposant," etc. In Proppian and Greimasian analysis the functions and roles of the actants occur at deep levels, and we are describing the encounter level as just beneath the surface level of the text, that is the unified, completed narrative flow. We have "bypassed" functions and actants because we believe that the semic approach we have employed here describes more accurately the precise composition of the narrative.

One might well describe these epics by means of functions and actants with the understanding that specific actions and characters develop at shallower levels of the text, but this formalist approach seems to us to add an unnecessary complication to the description of the text when one can begin directly with the semes which go into the make-up of the specific characters and encounters. Another advantage to explaining the flow of the narrative as based upon rules of action or narrative transforms is that we do not become enmeshed in functions operating in succession. Perhaps the epics could be explained in terms of successive functions, but this is not really necessary and the approach taken here allows, theoretically at least, for infinite possibilities of narrative change. With regard to functions, we find that one triggers another, which triggers another, and so on. The same thing, in fact, occurs with encounters, particularly where an encounter can generate the arrival of a given character, or where a character can bring about a certain encounter.[8] But, with encounters and rules of action we are not tied to a certain pattern. A character's response to a specific encounter can be explained on the basis of rules of action to be followed in specific situations. The major objection to what we are doing would undoubtedly be that the text is not conceived of on deep levels as elements of specific actions, rather that it is generated from general categories or structures with the specifics added in at higher levels. With this we would agree, but justly so, the principle of opposition is the general structure upon which specifics are built. Now, this in itself is too general to generate the Guillaume epics. It is the opposing apocalyptic and demonic images which offer the poems their uniqueness within the four-level structure we discussed in the previous chapter. That structure is the controlling element found deep within the genotext.[9] The semic level begins with the phenotext where the narrative process actually begins. That is to say, the four-level structure is not in fact part of the narrative per se but rather of the poetic conception of the epic. Were we to do so, it would be here that we would also identify such categories as functions and actants.

It is the rules of action operating as natural laws that really generate the movement of the narrative. The mere juxtaposition of characters and encounter situations will not create this movement unless there are directions as to how and where to move. In the Guillaume epics we discern three types of encounter situations, each one governed by a different set of narrative transforms:

> (1) common epic encounters comprising such "everyday" situations as meeting an enemy on the battlefield, preparing for battle, relating to a member of the opposite sex, relating to a colleague, etc.;

(2) encounters consisting of some ironic factor such as the use of a disguise, ruse, or dissimulation;

(3) encounters in which the archetypal images play a role.

Types (2) and (3) always apply to situations in which Guillaume is the principal character, with the one exception that Rainouart may also play the dominant role in certain circumstances. We will return to this. Type (1) may apply to any character including the hero.

The rules of action governing type (1) encounters are "intertextually" defined.[10] This is to say that the social and cultural background of the climate in which the text was produced will dictate the response of a character to an encounter. This means that pride, jealousy, nobility, loyalty, the various *chevaleresque* qualities of the epic world, will govern responses. Here "intertext" is broadly defined and relates not strictly to a textual tradition but to the larger environment in which the text is produced, but we shall return to this later. Examples of encounters of this type would be such things as Vivien's bravery in battle (*Guillaume* and *Aliscans*), Tedbald's cowardice (*Guillaume*), Guibourc's feeding the men and preparing an army while Guillaume is off at Archamps (*Guillaume*), and Rainouart's anger at being the butt of jokes while in Louis's kitchen (*Guillaume*).

In the example of Vivien's bravery it is easy to see that his response to Saracens on the battlefield will be to sacrifice himself if need be for the greater glory of France; he could not act in more "epic" a manner than this. Likewise we might define Guibourc's response to her husband's need for more men and supplies as a cultural one. She has not always been thought of in the most flattering terms perhaps, suggesting that she is a bit out of the ordinary for the wife of a knight, but while she may be somewhat out of the ordinary she does not have to seem anomalous. There were other strong women of the Middle Ages, doubtless many of them acting as real directive forces in male lives. Guibourc's efforts as a provider and helper are consonant with her royal station. As for Tedbald and Rainouart, their respective cowardice and anger certainly need not be seen as limited to their cultural contexts, but the responses of cowardly or angry persons to their respective situations carry them to logical ends. That is, Tedbald drives himself to ignominy as only a cowardly Frankish knight should, and Rainouart, the unrefined former Saracen, can only respond with brutal violence. These responses may seem obvious and it might be argued that the poet simply dictates the responses he wishes within the limits of *vraisemblance*. It is not simply authorial manipulation, however, that is in question here; rather, it is that these responses grow out of encounter situations which define the epic world as a genre, a world whose first concerns are war, bravery, the Crown, loyalty, etc. Thus, it is these encounters that can generate movement of the narrative. In this world, an encounter such as that between Guillaume and the bourgeois in the Val de Sigré episode of the *Moniage*, or between Bertran del Fossé and the gatekeeper of Paris during the Ysoré section of the same poem, does nothing to advance the narrative. Given the economy of line of the epics, there are, not surprisingly, few encounters which do not fit directly into the feudal-war axis of these poems.[11]

The rules of actions for type (2) encounters are of two kinds because of the ironic factor which defines this category. Subrule (1) dictates that the perpetrator, usually Guillaume, operates on the basis of some disjunction between what he is doing and what he intends. The disjunction itself may be of two kinds, that is to say doing, serving, or being one thing while in fact doing, saying, or being otherwise, or else simply not clearly identifying what is meant by what is done, said, or pretended. In other words, there is for the perpetrator some disjunction in time, space, or meaning between the response he makes to something and the effects of this response. Subrule (2) of this category of encounters says simply that the victim of the perpetrator's behavior responds to the encounter as if it were type (1), that is he responds seriously to it. Thus, the ironic situation. Examples of type (2) encounters include the *charroi* episode; Guillaume's disguise in the *Prise*; Rainouart himself in his battles with the Saracens; and the *braies*, Matamart, and destruction of the hermitage episodes in the *Moniage*.

The *charroi* episode and Guillaume's disguise in the *Prise* are obvious examples of an ironic situation based upon Guillaume's unrevealed knowledge of a fact which will ultimately make his adversaries unwitting victims. The latter act as if they take Guillaume to be a merchant and a messenger in those respective situations. Rainouart, however, is ironic on several counts for not only is he not immediately known to his former countrymen while he engages them in battle, but neither does he come off looking like the bumbling fool in these encounters that we might expect. Despite his appearance and recent past he has the inherent qualities of a knight. As for the examples of Guillaume in the *Moniage*, the *braies* episode is a perfect case of dramatic irony, the enemy totally unaware that they are being led into a trap. The hermitage destruction scene and the Matamart passage are much subtler. In the first, Guillaume fails to explain to Anseis why he behaves as he does, but he effectively prefigures symbolically what will happen to the Saracens even though he does not tell Anseis that he will ultimately go to Paris. In the second, Guillaume allows pretenders to the glory due the deliverer of Paris to expose themselves before being put down by one of the lowliest of creatures. In these two cases, as in all those of type (2) encounters, there is a marked disjunction between Guillaume's behavior and its results. Either a deception takes place so that a sudden and dramatic reversal can be effected, or the true significance of his behavior is hidden until such time as this significance can be revealed in a more dramatic fashion than were it to be revealed immediately.

Type (3) encounters, those in which archetypal images play a role, are the fewest in number but the most important. These obviously provide the major movement in the narration, the real *raison d'être* for the "petit cycle." It is expected, therefore, that Guillaume will be the principal character in these encounters, for he is the one influenced by these images. Yet, Rainouart can be found as the dominant character in Type (3) as in the bean field episode of the *Aliscans*. Here he takes on the semic qualities of Guillaume and responds to the wasteland image as would the latter; moreover, he, like Guillaume, is really concerned with the civilization goal at this point. Rainouart's assumption of what would otherwise be a role reserved exclusively for Guillaume occurs for several reasons. It is first a poetic means of reflecting upon the main motivational force behind the poem. Secondly, and perhaps more importantly, the assumption of such a role by a former Saracen, a lowly kitchen knave, highlights more dramatically than ever the idea of turning negative forces into positive ones, of creating a holistic, unified world out of one formerly and irretrievably divided. It is legitimate as well because Rainouart is in fact royalty, and in this world of the epic royalty is royalty so long as it can be made to serve one ideology.

Several comments about our three types of encounters. It is apparent that type (1) covers the greatest number of situations providing narrative movement. Type (2) is next in frequency; type (3) comprises the least number. The significance of these types, however, is that the overall value for the poem as a whole is in inverse proportion to frequency of occurrence. A great deal of repetition of type (3) examples is not necessary to draw attention to them so long as they are displayed effectively. Also, type (1) encounters relate only to themselves. That is, they generate narrative movement but do not relate, except in very general analogical ways, to other such encounters and movement. Type (2) encounters, however, possess a certain intratextuality, which is to say that they help to develop images or ideologies within a single text which go towards characterizing that text. Thus, Guillaume becomes associated with the *charroi* in disguise and ruse, and at the same time with the notion of cleansing by means of ruse. In the *Moniage* his attempts to withdraw from this world are underlined by his several ironic acts wherein his former image as a knight is less associated with his behavior. These type (2) encounters are therefore the source of much of the uniqueness of a particular text, its being easily and quickly identified by what takes place in such encounters. It is here also that the depth of character of Guillaume and Rainouart is developed. Type (3) encounters, then, are intratextual but also intertextual. They relate not only to what happens elsewhere in a given text but also to what happens in other texts of the cycle. As they are archetypally defined, they lift the text from a purely cultural or social level of meaning to the mythic level, and as they are the primary generators of narrative movement they tend to mythify in imagistic form not only the principal character (Guillaume, but to a certain extent Rainouart, too) but the ideology of the poems as well. We can say, therefore, that while the three types of encounters all provide horizontal movement within the narrative, types (2) and (3) also have paradigmatic properties, type (2) mildly so, type (3) strongly so. Ironically, the strong forces generating the narrative flow also tend to stop it. Along with the retardative influence of iconic and indexical signs, the three types of encounters tend to compete with one another in pushing and halting the epic narrative.

At this point we have a generated narrative, a text. As we have shown, it is a text composed of syntagmatic and paradigmatic elements which compete with each other for the progression and stopping of the narrative flow. And as we have also seen, the strong forces primarily responsible for pushing the narrative on are also responsible for stopping it and creating the static images which we associate with medieval epics. This brings us to some other questions of "paradigmaticity" or of intertextuality, that is the notions of mythic images, hypersign, and macrotext.

We have already used the term intertextuality as Kristeva does in *Le texte du roman* to signify the social and cultural background of the era in which a text is produced. This is a broad use of the term, but a legitimate one, indicating that intertextuality relates not only to texts as such but to other media as well. It also indicates that it is possible to understand the aspects or effects of intertextuality as shifting from one medium to another.[12] In referring strictly to texts, however, I intend the term intertext to mean what Laurent Jenny has called it: "[le] texte absorbant une multiplicité de textes tout en restant centré par un sens" ("La stratégie de la forme").

The intertext of the Guillaume poems is where the mythic qualities of these poems reside. It is that space both from which the individual poems are generated via the skill of the poet and to which the multiple images of Guillaume and his mission flow from the various poems in contributing to the complete mythic images of these texts. Thus, the intertext is in a constant state of revision or recomposition so long as these oral poems remain alive in the mouths of poet-*jongleurs*. There is nothing fixed about this intertext during the era of the epics; it is composed of infinite possibilities, but its actual poetic space is being constantly redefined and limited within the confines offered to it by the semic nature of individual texts. It is for that reason that we cannot "know" Guillaume through any one text, but only through the intertext.

These poems generate two primary mythic images from and for the intertext although it is difficult to separate the one from the other. The first is the image of Guillaume himself as epic hero/civilizer; the other is the "verb" Guillaume, that is his mission, his central concerns, those essential actions which define the message of the text. Here, again, we find the two essential ingredients for the narrative, an "actant" and a predicate, but here, again, we must also remember that the central action of these texts becomes an atemporal static image. We find, therefore, that in following the complete circle of the life and generation of a text from intertext, to deep structure, to surface structure, and all the way back up to the intertext again, the binary principle of opposition is the controlling force. The medieval epic is a narrative contradiction in a permanent state of disjunction: it moves and yet is does not; it operates on a temporal plane of chronology and causality, and yet it is constantly bidding for an atemporal space where its myth can be apprehended and decoded.

Our term "mythic image" has a relationship to some other terms which have also intertextual properties, terms such as hypersign, supersign, and macrotext. Hypersign is a term used by Maria Corti in *An Introduction to Literary Semiotics* to describe the text as a whole, that is the total or global meaning of the text which is not absolutely the sum of the meanings of the words and their enunciations. This is related to what Eco calls a supersign-function (*A Theory of Semiotics* 271). Here the hypersign would really have to be equated with the complex of two types of mythic images we have mentioned above, that is with both the actant and the verb. Corti then carries this intertextual aspect one step further introducing the concept of the macrotext. This she defines as a large unitary text, the configuration of which is composed of one author's collection of poems, and the text of each of which is a microstructure articulated inside a macrostructure or the functional and informative character of the collection.

> It is like saying that the total meaning does not coincide with the sum of the partial meanings of single texts, but goes beyond it...The functionality and information possibility of a collection as such occurs when at least one of the following conditions is present: (1) if there exists a combination of thematic and/or formal elements that runs through all the texts and produces the unity of the collection; (2) if there is a progression to the discourse for which each single text can occupy only one place. (112)

Corti clearly intends this to apply to one author, but we affirm here that it is also applicable to the Guillaume poems. The shared poetic consciousness of these epics is such that they could well have been done by one author even though it is obvious they were not. Moreover, it is doubtful as to how important authorship really was with respect to the epics. Nevertheless, it is quite evident that both conditions (1) and (2) are satisfied by the Guillaume poems. The first is patently obvious at this point. As for the second, it must be said that we do not find in our cycle that each text occupies a specific place in a progression. With the exception of the *Moniage*, it would not matter greatly which poems were read first, even though, for example, it is clear when reading the *Prise* that the *Charroi* was intended to precede it, or that the *Couronnement* is to precede them both. There is generally not all that much chronicity to Old French epics; what matters is the mosaic obtained by the end of a poem or in this case, of the Cycle. But there is only one space for each of these poems in the macrotext, for each one has a function to perform, atemporally, in making it up. We equate macrotext with our use of the term intertext and mention it here because we feel that the compositional notion of it is essential to the understanding of the intertext, and because it demonstrates again the remarkable reliability achieved by the various poets responsible for this uniquely coherent collection of texts.

One point remains to be said regarding intertextuality. As the archetypal images help to establish an intertextual relationship with other texts, and as they lift the text from a cultural, social level of meaning to the mythic level, we see that they do so as symbolic unities which are unities of restriction:

> Le symbole assume le symbolisé [les universaux] comme irréductible au symbolisant [les marques]. La pensée mythique qui tourne dans l'orbite du symbol et qui se manifeste dans l'épopée, les contes populaires, les chansons de geste, etc. opère avec des unités symboliques qui sont des UNITES DE RESTRICTION par rapport aux universaux symbolisées ["l'héroisme", "le courage", "la noblesse", "la vertu", "la peur", "la trahison", etc.]. La fonction du symbole est donc, dans sa dimension verticale [universaux-marques] une fonction de RESTRICTION. (Kristeva. *Le texte du roman* 26-27)

That is, there is no room for ambivalence. What is symbolized is a whole and complex entity or concept, an either/or, a well-defined this or that. The space of the symbol is totally restricted or completely defined. This has value on several levels for not only does it mean that there is no ambiguity as to meaning of the text, but it also has psychological and aesthetic value.

In discussing the framework of literary composition, Juri Lotman states that in giving shape to a limitless object such as reality by means of a finite text, it is in fact impossible to represent only part of the life represented, that inevitably this life in its entirety is represented. Although one might wish to represent a limited object such as the destiny of Anna Karenina, this object reflects the destiny of all women, of all men of this social and cultural era. He postulates, therefore, that there are two aspects to the modeling of a text: the mythological, which refers to the entire universe, and the fabulous, which refers to some specific aspect of reality (*La structure du texte artistique* 302). Given that the Guillaume poems are exclusively mythic in nature, and given that we expect them to deal with a total human experience on a universal level such as civilization, we further expect to find these texts whole, complete, and well defined like the symbols used in their composition. By this we mean that the literary space of these poems is complete and unambiguous. The author manipulates extraordinary archetypal images in order to focus upon a civilization goal and to communicate a particular and unambiguous meaning. He is also interested, as an author, in pure manipulation of symbols for their own sake. But since the symbols, archetypes, and mythic images of the epic world are all complete, well defined, and unambiguous, we find that this manipulation results in the creation of a well-defined literary and psychological space which is satisfying in itself. A sense of wholeness or completion is thus achieved not only in terms of the message of the text but also in terms of its purely literary elements. We shall return to this in a chapter on spatial relationships. Suffice it to say here that the very notion of intertextuality with respect to mythic texts means that there is a conscious effort not only to unify texts with one another but also to define their poetic space as wholly and as completely as possible.

Chapter Four

Time

—Turc m'ont cachié bien pres d'une jornee
(*Aliscans* 1830)

—De lor jornees ne vos sai aconter
(*Couronnement* 279)

—Succession, flux, change...seem to belong to the most immediate and primitive data of our experience, and they are aspects of time. There is no experience, as it were, which does not have a temporal index attached to it. (Hans Meyerhoff. *Time in Literature* 1)

Old French epics tend either to be very specific about time or incapable of being at all specific about it; an event takes a specified length of time or perhaps just "a long time." Perhaps there is nothing odd about that. Add to it, however, the fact that time in general appears to be circular in the epic, that is to say that we are dealing here with mythic time or a sense of timelessness, and the fact that there does not appear to be any particular logic to the measurement of time when it is measured nor any particular reason to measure certain events and not others, then epic temporality becomes something of a puzzle. How, when, or why should it be measured, and what is the effect of measuring or not measuring time? These are questions to be dealt with in this chapter as one further step in the process of defining the overall epic sphere of the Cycle de Guillaume and in defining the relationship between audience and text.

A number of issues need to be dealt with in approaching time, and time is no easy question in any realm, let alone the Old French epic. Time may be seen as change, as motion or movement of bodies in space, as a series of points laid out in space, or as nonspatial duration. It may be conceived of as linear or as circular, as a state of mind, or as a function of memory or anticipation. It is an elusive concept which takes us back to Augustine and beyond to the ancient Greeks, and then returns us again to modern writers and philosophers such as Bergson and Proust. Our understanding of time can be as fleeting as the thing itself.

The Greeks are credited with having conceived of time in the West as cyclical or as eternal repetition.[1] Time for them was seen as a threat, not as a continual evolution but as a threatening change. The Greek tragedy of the fifth century was tightly time-bound, concerned with the rhythm of an action closely linked to the twenty-four-hour day. The epic also dealt with time, or change, or contrasts between the before and after, but it was not linked to any specific time limit. Epics were settled in an indeterminate past, a past that could be seen as an ever-present reality. Past and present could thus become fused, a characteristic that is found in the Old French epic. As for Greek myth, of course, it belongs to no precise or determinate time; it is ever-present as well as set in an indeterminate past. This, too will be reflected in the *chansons de geste*.

Moving forward a bit we find St. Augustine (*Confessions, Book XI*) concerned with some very specific problems related to our understanding of time: the relative length or measurement of an action or experience in time; the nonexistence of past or future times because they have ceased to be or have not yet come into being; the measurement of periods of time as they go by but are not yet in the past. For Augustine, the past and the future are really memory and expectation; only present time, as it is experienced at the moment that it is passing, can really be said to have any existence at all. Augustine therefore leads us to the conclusion that present time itself is of such short existence that what we do largely in conceiving of "time" is to deal in memory and expectation.

Closer to our own era is Bergson's notion of duration offering a considerably different view of time (*Essai sur les données immédiates de la conscience*). Bergson was concerned with defining duration, which really has to do with the present. Here he affirms that it consists of a succession of qualitative changes which fuse with one another, a series of states of consciousness that are inseparable from one another and that are not given to any symbolic representation which is in any way spatial. Thus, the time of duration is purely qualitative and in no way quantitative—it is an ever-present state of consciousness which does not distinguish itself from its former states and which cannot, in fact, be measured.

Thus, time calls up a multiplicity of concerns. Perhaps Hans Meyerhoff has best summed up these concerns as the following characteristics of time in literature throughout the ages:

(1) subjective relativity, or unequal distribution of time

(2) continuous flow, or duration

(3) dynamic fusion, or interpenetration, of the causal order in experience and memory

(4) duration and the temporal structure of memory in relation to self-identity

(5) eternity

(6) transitoriness, or the temporal direction toward death (foreknowledge of death)

Says Meyerhoff, "These six are descriptions which translate into abstract language what the literary portrait depicts and explicates in the specific case and concrete situation. They are abstract concepts about certain qualitative aspects of time in human experience which do not find a place in the construction of an axiomatic system of time in nature" (133). But, let us be more specific about expressions of time in the Middle Ages.

We know that medieval man was much closer to nature than we are today, and that consequently he tended to be in touch with the rhythm of the seasons and days. Given the imprecise nature of these units of time, and the fact that a "day" in winter was of different length from a "day" in summer, these units were only approximations at best. As Marc Bloch points out, man was simply ill-equipped to measure time and the determination of an exact hour or the age of someone necessarily became a subject of discussion and debate (*Feudal Society* 72-75). It is thus fair to say, as Bloch does, that there was a vast indifference to time, that the passage of time escaped man's grasp, and that a concern for accuracy in measuring time with the aid of figures was totally alien to him.

Nor, apparently, did man feel the need to measure time, leaving its concern up to God. In *The Renaissance Discovery of Time*, Ricardo Quinones notes that "For the Middle Ages time could be abundant, because behind the chances and changes of events man could sense a higher directing order.... Because of his fate he could then exist in an attitude of temporal ease. Neither time nor change appear to be critical, and hence there is no great worry about controlling the future" (7).

Georges Poulet puts it another way by saying that for the Christian of the Middle Ages there was no difference between existence and duration, or that there was no sense of becoming or changing (*Etudes sur le temps humain* i). In other words, created beings are in a constant state of creation, not a state of renewal. But Poulet also emphasizes, as does Quinones, that all "time" came from God and that it was directed by Him. Thus, change as we usually think of it, that is altered states which we measure quantitatively or in spatial terms, is alien to the Christian of this period. Man therefore feels himself as a being having duration.

There are other aspects of medieval temporality as well. First, let us note that "duration" as we have just used it does not suggest the smooth flow of time, but refers rather to a Bergsonian ever-present, a concept to which we shall return. In addition, we can say that any succession was not viewed spatially, at least in the early Middle Ages up to the advent of clocks (which first appeared in Germany around 1200), but was rather experienced rhythmically. Thus the notion of circularity, the "eternal return," and thus, again, the notion of an ever-present. Such a concept of time binds tightly our notion of the past to the present, but it also tightly links the future to the present. The future was a world of unlimited possibilities, and which, as we shall see in the epics, had a connotation of something willed. Will and intention could therefore lend some stability to the future and tend to lessen its uncertainty. Or, we might say that what happens in the future, especially where what happens has already been determined as "right" by the ethical framework of the poem, is really a function of the past or present. The future, therefore, is really not seen as a spatially differentiated period of time separate from the past or present, but is instead a state of actualized possibility or potentiality. As Richard Glasser has said: "The element of continuity between today and tomorrow was a matter of one's mental attitude, not a conscious extension of what has been and what is"(*Time in French Life and Thought* 36).

Duration in the Middle Ages had highly emotional overtones. Glasser tells us again that an expression such as *il m'est tart* indicated a soul-state or a feeling about a situation. We will find that in epic poetry an expression of impatience suggests not a desire that the future arrive as we might say today, but rather a response to inner stress, a desire for things to be as they should. Desire and fulfillment are really temporally unseparated, Glasser insists; "to wish to fight" is "to fight." Thus, we will also see that certain temporal formulae, such as *ja mais*, may be used to convey an intensity of feeling more than a sense of differentiated time. Many indications of time in the early epic are used to convey atmosphere and thus have no real temporal function. Time in the epic, therefore, may be a highly personal and subjective phenomenon.

As for general appraisals of time in the *chanson de geste*, they tend to reflect what the foregoing have indicated. Paul Zumthor notes that there is really no beginning nor end to the action of the epic, that the hero and his *gestes* exist in the collective memory of the audience (*Essai de poétique médiévale* 322-28). The epic, he says, really escapes time and becomes a conscience of itself where the real subject of the action is collectivity. Thus, all is present, actual, giving rise to the poem's great "moral model" function and indicating the latent allegorical nature of the epic.

Karl Uitti seems to echo the views of Zumthor. He describes space and time as magical in the *Roland* and as both visibly and potentially confused principally because of the dovetailing of thematic material as seen, for example, in the foreshadowing of Roland's death. "Chronologies," says Uitti, "are disturbed, indeed made light of, as are the locations of actions and their consequences.... Normal sequential chronologies are simply less important than the authentic temporality of the poem: *aevum*, of course, and what might be called the 'concrete' time of events—a time possessing its own relational logic. Thus, Roland's death takes place in a diachrony that presumably extends back earlier than the duration of the poem: a blood feud? Its synchrony encompasses at least the Roncevaux episode if not the entire poem. As an event, it exists in relation to other 'events' " (*Old French Narrative Poetry: story, myth, celebration* 121-22). Thus, Uitti, too, seems to focus not only upon the characteristics of change and no change, but also upon the idea that the poem's temporality is defined, at least in part, by a notion of collectivity, or in this case a logic of events existing outside of time.

William Calin offers yet a different view of time in the epics from what we have mentioned so far, and insists that a clear continuum and change can, in fact, be found in selected cases. In *The Old French Epic of Revolt* he points out that the general tendency of the epic is to compress time and to offer little opportunity for character development. This is the case with the *Roland*, the *Chanson de Guillaume*, and the *Gormont et Isembard* with the one exception that Isembard can be seen to change with time from rebel to saint. With regard to *Raoul de Cambrai*, however, Calin takes issue with Bloch's thesis that the Middle Ages were necessarily and inevitably imprecise in matters of time for he shows clearly that this poem is remarkably precise and consistent with respect to chronology. Moreover, he demonstrates that the listener becomes conscious of the thirty years of war and suffering and that the personnages involved develop in time and are subject to change. The same can be said for *Renaud de Montauban*. In this poem, however, we also return to chronological inconsistencies as a result of composition by many poets and the subsequent influence of *remanieurs* and scribes, but Calin still insists upon the symbolic value of time (i.e., change, duration) as just as important here as in *Raoul*. "In all of the revolt epics," he says, "time serves as a very real continuum, the essential prerequisite without which growth would be impossible, without which characters such as Bernier, Renaud, and Girard would never come to grips with their juridical problems and find a solution" (195).

For the most part, time in the Middle Ages has been viewed as something unmeasured by comparison with the modern clock-bound world, as controlled by the rhythm of the seasons and the span of a life, as an ever-present devoid of change and becoming, and as something related to states of feeling or states of being. These views have been largely supported by general assessments of time in the epics with the *caveat* that there indeed can be found expressions of change, development or growth in some of these poems.

What is needed now is a systematic study of time in the epics which will allow not only verification of the observations mentioned above but also an understanding of the aesthetics involved in the temporality of these poems. The obvious problem, however, is one of establishing a sound approach because the various aspects of literary temporality are numerous indeed, and only a few have ever been treated with any rigor.

Time in the epic may be approached from several different directions: the point of view of the narrator, the point of view of the listener, tense usage, adverbs, certain stylistic features which can create the impression of flux or stasis, flashback and foreshadowing, repetition and ellipsis. Or it might be instructive and convenient to follow an approach such as one of those which have already been outlined for modern narrative as in Harald Weinrich's *Le temps* or in Gérard Genette's *Figures III*. The obvious problem with either of the latter, however, is that we are not dealing with modern narrative, and while it would be possible to pick and choose what we can use for medieval narrative we might not profit greatly. Moreover, both Weinrich and Genette depend to a great extent upon what would be called point of view, and while that certainly is to be considered in due course, it may not be all that crucial for an initial understanding of epic time.

To characterize time in the Guillaume poems is to determine whether or not there is a sense of temporality, whether or not there appears or does not appear to be any "time." What we are really asking is whether or not we can appreciate any sense of change in time or whether there is any stasis or flux. We have already noted above that change and stasis may both be found in the epic, but even this determination is insufficient as a basis for our study of time for it cannot take into account problems of inconsistency in chronology or the outright contradictions of time often found in the epics.

Another consideration that must be made is how time is perceived by the listener of the poem. There are two kinds of time, or perhaps we should say two kinds of perception of time: objective and subjective. By objective we mean standardized or measurable time, that is "clock time" where every day contains twenty-four equal hours, every hour sixty equal minutes, etc. Subjective time is not standardized but approximated time or time judged unscientifically (unobjectively?) against some previous measure of time existing in our memory. What we are dealing with in the Guillaume poems is subjective time to the virtual exclusion of the objective kind. There is simply no way that we can honestly objectify what happens in the epic nor claim that we have a temporally objective view of what takes place. All of our temporal perceptions are measured against something else in the poem. Yet the problem then remains of determining what our "standard" is so that we can say that time is passing and how fast or slow it is progressing.

It may nevertheless be impossible to choose such a standard. Where are we then? Back where we started with the simple feeling that sometimes we sense a movement in time and that sometimes we do not. That is really the place we should start. It is there that we should establish our base for a study of epic temporality insisting on nothing more than a differentiation between movement and nonmovement in time. What this really means is that we are sometimes aware of time passing and that sometimes we are not. Now if we consider time from this aspect, then we do not need to worry yet about such things as inconsistencies or contradictions, for perception of these things simply means that we are consciously aware of time itself regardless of whether or not it follows any logical chronological pattern. We can sort out later the significance or effects, if any, of problems in chronology. Likewise any consideration of the speed or change in speed of time can be subsumed under this general distinction of the mere perception of temporality.

The other half of this distinction in epic time is the absence of any perception of temporality, that is to say that state in which we are unaware of any sense of time in the poem at all. Either we are aware of time or we are not. It seems difficult for us today to imagine being unaware of time because of our adherence to the clock and because our lives are well regulated to some commonly accepted standard. Usually we can tell the time of day to within a few minutes during our waking hours even without a clock. We operate with a time consciousness barely submerged beneath the surface of our primary consciousness. This was certainly not the case with medieval man, and it most assuredly, therefore, was not a situation to be found in the literature of the period. In fact, there is evidence in the epic that both the poet and the listener "lost track" of time as we know it or lost consciousness of the flow of time regardless of how logical the flow might have been. This is the state that Bergson identified as "duration," or nonspatial time, and it is one that poets were cleverly able to use in order to manipulate their audiences and to create certain desired effects. Epic states of duration occur in moments of great emotional intensity or at points of high listener involvement with the action of the poem where one is no longer conscious of the passage or marking off of time. This nonspatial time is, however, constantly interrupted by spatial time or anything which draws attention to the passage or to the marking of time in such a way that discrete units of time are appreciated. As will become apparent, the temporal style of the epic is basically durational. This is due partly to its mythic nature, and partly to the use of certain stylistic features.

The Guillaume poems utilize a combination of five techniques in creating either spatial or nonspatial temporality: (1) manipulation of tenses,

(2) distortion of chronology, (3) epic formulas, (4) isolated temporal expressions such as adverbs and conjunctions, and (5) an appositional mode. Tenses are most often used to create nonspatial time as is the infrequent but effective appositional mode. The remaining techniques tend to generate a sense of spatial time, although tenses may also be manipulated to that end.

I. Tenses.

Most of the few studies done on time in medieval French literature, have focused upon tense usage.[2] The major points which they have made are: that the present is the dominant epic tense; that the imperfect is rarely used in this genre, and then principally for such things as a shift to secondary material or to the *vraisemblable* but not the actual (the present often being used in an imperfect aspect to show repeated action, temperament, or to characterize permanent states); that the preterite and perfect can also be used in a present aspect, with the perfect often alternating with the present to describe central concerns, and the preterite used for background or for central concerns which are to be given some finality or authority as a future; and that the *passé composé* can be used as a future anterior. These observations tend to substantiate widely held feelings that the epic is composed in a "present consciousness" or an ever-present aspect which extends back into history and forward into the future, fixed and unchanging. They suggest collaterally that what has been, is still, and will ever be, or that what will be already is and was predetermined long ago. In our opinion, the work of Stefenelli-Fürst is the most thorough treatment of individual tenses although the others mentioned below have certainly made highly valuable contributions as well. But one of the most revealing studies to date is that of Rupert Pickens whose concern is historical versus ahistorical writing in medieval literature.[3] Pickens convincingly demonstrates how a literary work should be analyzed according to its diegetic and mimetic parts while analyzing the kinds of tenses used in each. Normally we would expect diegesis to be composed of historical tenses while mimesis would largely be composed of the "present" tenses. Pickens clearly shows that this is not always the case, but perhaps more importantly he offers a valuable procedure for analyzing tense usage.

Table I

DIEGESIS

	Past Absolute	%	Past Perfect	%	Imp.	%	Passé Composé	%	Preterite	%	Present	%	Cond.	%	Future	%	TOTAL
Guillaume	33	1.74	9	.48	49	2.59	261	13.80	705	37.26	811	42.87	0	0	24	1.27	1892
Aliscans	162	2.35	101	1.46	426	6.18	1134	16.44	2095	30.37	2788	40.42	27	.39	165	2.39	6898
Couronnement	19	1.35	12	.85	87	6.19	205	14.60	432	30.75	626	44.56	5	.36	19	1.35	1405
Charroi	10	1.78	4	.71	38	6.76	86	15.30	161	28.65	236	41.99	4	.71	23	4.09	562
Prise	23	2.57	6	.67	25	2.80	112	12.53	264	29.53	427	47.76	1	.11	36	4.03	894
Moniage	83	2.12	47	1.20	251	6.42	609	15.57	856	21.89	1925	49.22	19	.49	121	3.09	3911

MIMESIS

	Past Absolute	%	Past Perfect	%	Imp.	%	Passé Composé	%	Preterite	%	Present	%	Cond.	%	Future	%	TOTAL
Guillaume	37	1.83	19	.94	87	4.31	210	10.41	248	12.30	1033	51.21	71	3.52	312	15.47	2017
Aliscans	19	.42	57	1.26	213	4.69	524	11.54	410	9.03	2387	52.59	127	2.80	802	17.67	4539
Couronnement	7	.50	4	.29	71	5.06	90	6.42	178	12.70	812	57.92	44	3.14	196	13.98	1402
Charroi	9	.94	16	1.66	51	5.30	104	10.81	153	15.90	489	50.83	27	2.81	113	11.75	962
Prise	4	.4	4	.4	63	6.30	80	8.0	123	12.30	503	50.30	54	5.40	169	16.9	1000
Moniage	12	.36	15	.45	173	5.23	213	6.44	302	9.12	1823	55.08	109	3.29	663	20.03	3310

In Table I (opposite page) is shown the distribution of tenses in the diegetic and mimetic parts of each of our six poems.[4] A quick overview will confirm what has been said before which is that the present accounts for the largest percentage of the verbal structure of the epic. Also, as anticipated, we find that relatively few imperfects are used and that after the present tense, the perfects and preterites comprise the next largest group. It is particularly interesting to note the distribution of tenses within the diegetic and mimetic parts of the texts.

The present accounts for 50.30% to 57.92% of the mimetic portion while it makes up 40.42% to 49.22% in the diegetic part; the difference between the two may range from not quite 3% to as much as over 13%. The perfect accounts for 12.5% to almost 16.5% in diegesis while it comprises not quite 6.5% to 11.5% in mimesis with a difference of approximately 3% to 9% between the two in any given poem. If we are to insist upon the perfect as a "present" tense then we would expect the higher percentage of perfects to appear in mimesis—unless, of course, we can account for a higher percentage in diegesis as a result of commentative text, which is precisely the case. Assuming commentary to make up roughly 1% of the text as suggested by Pickens, this reduces the figures for diegesis somewhat but still leaves diegesis with a higher percentage than mimesis.[5] Since this is the case for every poem without exception, we can only assume, in the Guillaume poems at least, that this is the norm but that the perfect is as important to diegesis, if not slightly more so, than it is to mimesis. It may still be a "present" tense but it is apparently more valuable as description or as a substitute for the future anterior where what is to come is already a *fait accompli*.

The other "present" tenses behave as expected. The conditional accounts for 0% to only .71% in diegesis while it is a minimum of 2.81% to a maximum of 5.4% in mimesis with a spread of from 2.4% to 5.3%. The future makes up anywhere from 1.35% to 4.09% in diegesis and 11.75% to 20.03% in mimesis with differences between 7.6% and 17%. The conditional is of little real use in the epic where there is little speculation, doubt, or question about anything. As for the future, its predominance in mimesis is not surprising where it is often used in boasting. Furthermore, it is important to note that in every case the future accounts for a higher percentage of mimesis than does the perfect, suggesting the importance of the elements of desire in mimetic text. This is to say that how things should or shall be is more important than how they are presently or that how they should be is more important than the issue of description.

The past tenses hold no real surprises at all. The imperfect accounts for no more than 6.76% of diegesis, 6.3% of mimesis. The preterite is predictably heavier in diegesis than mimesis with a range of 21.89% to 37.26% as opposed to 9.03% to 15.9%. The pluperfect is about equally represented in both portions of our texts, but only minimally at that—in the neighborhood of 1%—while the past absolute has a slightly heavier use in diegesis (1.35% to 2.57%) than in mimesis (.36% to 1.83%). The pluperfect and past absolute are so minimal, and within a fairly constant range, as to be insignificant in the total scheme of things except to say that the kind of historicizing they represent is of little use in the epic. That is, there is apparently no need to embed events that far back into the past in epic narrative for, again, there is no real distinction between the three temporal segments of "past," "present," and "future" as we would think of them.

Table II

	Total Poem	Diegesis	% Dieg.	Mimesis	% Mim.
Guillaume	3909	1892	48.40	2017	51.60
Aliscans	11437	6898	60.31	45.39	39.69
Couronnement	2807	1405	50.05	1402	49.95
Charroi	1524	562	36.88	962	63.12
Prise	1894	894	47.20	1000	52.80
Moniage	7221	3911	54.16	3310	45.84

Time 73

Looking at our figures as a whole, we find in Table II that diegesis accounts for a minimum of 36.88% and a maximum of 60.31%. Mimesis accounts for between 39.69% and 63.12%. In the case of the *Chanson de Guillaume*, the *Charroi de Nîmes*, and the *Prise d'Orange,* mimesis is greater than diegesis, the reverse being true for *Aliscans*, the *Couronnement de Louis*, and the *Moniage Guillaume*. Nevertheless, all of the poems are clearly "ahistorical" in the way Pickens uses the term: "the abundance of mimesis makes them dramatic by comparison with other kinds of compositions, and events are recounted more often with the same sense of immediacy and subjective involvement by the narrator as if taking place at the present moment or having occurred very recently, than with objective, historical detachment" (173).

We now have statistical evidence to support the notion that epic poetry is composed in an "epic present," and it appears that the choice of tenses is quite regular in this genre regardless of the obvious multiplicity of poets and redactors.[6] Before leaving this point, however, a few comments are in order. In counting the verbs of the Guillaume poems we have chosen not to include such phrases as *dist-il* because this does not reveal anything about the temporal structure of the narrative. What matters is what is said and the tense in which it is said. It must also be noted that certain tenses may obviously be chosen because of verse length or assonance requirements. Thus, it may be that in one context the preterite is appropriate whereas in another only the perfect will satisfy.[7] Furthermore, certain verbs seem always to be used in a particular tense. In the *Chanson de Guillaume*, for example, we find the perfect *ad acraventi*, but it is rarely, if ever, found in the preterite form of the verb. When an infrequently used tense does occur, such as the pluperfect, it tends to be repeated several times (see vv. 6793-96 of the *Aliscans*) unless it is a pluperfect subjunctive (*Aliscans* 6887) or some such awkward construction. Despite these facts, however, tense usage overall is quite regular. Of concern to us now is how tenses may function to give the impression of spatial time or of duration.

For the most part duration is that state which is created by verbs in the present tense with no pointed reference to any other period of time, a state in which the listener becomes involved in the action of the poem either because he can associate closely with it or simply because he manages to be caught by the spirit of the moment. He can be brought back to a temporal consciousness by a number of techniques, but with respect to tense usage this usually means a shift from present to past (and often from mimesis into diegesis) in such a way that the image before him becomes separated from him, frozen, or spatialized mentally. Yet, duration does not have to be broken by the use of a past tense even in the midst of a passage where the present predominates. The use of the preterite and perfect in the following passage in fact are used to emphasize important facts in a very "present" context, and they in no way spatialize the text.

> Dunc li vestirent une broine mult bele
> E un vert healme li lacent en la teste;
> Dunc ceint s'espee, le brant burni vers terre,
> Une grant targe i tint par manevele;
> Espiet trenchant si out en sa main destre,
> E blanche enseigne li lacent tresqu'a tere.
> Dunc li ameinent un cheval de Chastele:
> Munte Tidbalz par sun estrieu senestre;
> Si'n est issu par une des posternes,
> Al dos le siwent dis mil d'homes od helmes.
> En Larchamp vont rei Deramed requere.
> (*Chanson de Guillaume* 133-43)[8]

Likewise, in the following passage the vivid action and emotional tension of the moment are composed by the present and preterite, creating a state of duration:

> Dunc met sa main en sa vermeille chalce,
> Si traist tut fors une enseigne de paille;
> A treis clous d'or l'afermat en sa lance,
> Od le braz destre en ad brandi la hanste,
> Desi qu'az poinz l'en batirent les langues.
> Point le cheval, ne pot muer ne saille,
> Fiert un paien desur sa doble targe:
> Tute li fent de l'un ur desqu'a l'altre;
> Trenchat le braz qui li sist en l'enarme,
> Colpe le piz e trenchad la coraille,
> Par mi l'eschine sun grant espiet li passe,
> Tut estendu l'abat mort en la place.
> Crie: "Munjoi!", ço fu l'enseigne Charle.
> (*Chanson de Guillaume* 315-27)

Another example of a well-created state of duration may be found in this passage in the *Couronnement:*

> Hé! Deus, aïde!" dist li cuens Fierebrace,
> "Onc mais nuls clers nen ot le cuer si large!
> Or ne laireie, por nul ome que sache,
> Ne por paien, tant seit ne fel ne aspres,
> A cels glotons ne me voise combatre.
> Bels niés Bertrans, alez prendre vos armes,
> Et Guielins et li altre barnages."
> Armes demande Guillelmes Fierebrace;
> On li aporte devant lui en la place.
> Il vest l'alberc et le vert elme lace,
> Et ceint l'espee par les renges de paile.
> On li ameine le balcent en la place;
> Li cuens i monte, que il estrier n'i baille.
> A son col pent une vermeille targe,
> Entre ses poinz un reit espié qui taille,
> A cinc clos d'or gonfanon i atache:
> "Sire apostoiles", dist Guillelmes li sages,
> "Combien avez de gent en vostre marche?"
> Dist apostoiles: "Jel vos dirai sens faille:
> Trei mile somes, n'i a cel n'ait ventaille,
> Et fort espié, et espee qui taille."
> Respont li cuens: "C'est bele començaille.
> Armer les faites, et tote la pietaille,
> Qui nos tendront les portes et les barres."
> Et cil respont: "Bien est dreiz qu'on la face."
> Par tote Rome s'arote li barnages.
> Quant armé furent, si vindrent en la place.
> Li apostoiles lor a fait un seignacle:
> "Seignor baron", dist l'apostoiles sages,
> "Qui en cest jor morra en la bataille
> En paradis avra soin herberjage,
> Que nostre sire a ses bons amis guarde;
> Sainz Gabriëls li sera guionages."
> Lors se leverent, chascuns saisi ses armes
> Envers la gent orgoillose et salvage.
> Si come il vindrent, hurtent par lor oltrage
> A la grant porte, qui n'esteit mie basse:
> "Seignor baron," dist l'apostoiles sages,

> "Ici endreit guarderez cest barnage;
> J'irai parler a l'amirant Galafre;
> Se por aveir que promettre li sache
> Vuelt retorner et ses nes et ses barges,
> Et ses granz oz, qui ci sont demorables,
> Je li donrai le grant tresor de l'arche;
> N'i demorra ne calices ne chape,
> Ors ne argenz ne qui un denier vaille.
> Ainz qu'il i muire tant gentill ome sage."
> (*Couronnement de Louis* 398-444)

These examples demonstrate how the past tenses can be combined with the present to maintain duration. There are also cases where the future appears but in such a way that it seems to be almost continuous with the present:

> Tedbalz demande: "Que feruns, Viviëns?"
> Ço dist li bers: "Ne ferum el que bien!"
> "Sire Tedbalz", dist Viviëns li ber,
> "Vus estes quons e si mult honurez
> Des meillurs homes de rivage de mer.
> Si m'en creez, ne serras ja blasmez.
> Pren tes messages, fai tes amis mander!
> N'obliëz mie dan Guillelme al cur nes!
> Sages hom est en bataille champel:
> Il la set bien maintenir e garder;
> Se il i vient, nus veintrums Deramed!"
> (*Chanson de Guillaume* 48-58)

> Dist li portiers: "Certes vus n'enterez
> Ainceis l'avrai a ma dame cunté.
> Va dunc, amis gardez ne demorez!"
> (*Chanson de Guillaume* 2218-20)

In the following verse from *Aliscans*, the present is used in a future sense, suggesting again that what is to come has already achieved the status of the actual:

> Nos le ravrons ains ke past le tiers dis.
> (*Aliscans* 4169)

In the following example the future tense is used with a sense of immediacy to bring that which is about to happen right into the present, and consequently with some measure of haste and some slight emotional tension:

> Dist Rainouars: "Aparmain le savrés,
> Ja voir por toi nen ert mes noms celés.
> Rainouars sui et d'Espaigne sui nes.
> (*Aliscans* 6359-60)

In no case such as these does the future have any real future sense, that is as something spatially set apart from the present or even the past. The future is already fact, present fact for that matter, so we can say once again that a mode of continuity is developed wherein past, present, and future are indistinguishable one from the other and wherein duration is therefore established.

We have just seen examples where past, present, and future tenses can create or maintain duration. On the other hand, it is possible to find cases where time becomes spatialized and yet where there are more presents than, say, pasts as in this passage from the *Chanson de Guillaume* where direct reference to the time of day and its passage creates a distancing between listener and text:

> Clers fu lu jurz e bels fu li matins;
> Li soleiz raied, si'st li jurz esclariz.
> Paien devalent par un broilled antif.
> Par unt qu'il passent tote terre fremist,
> E des durs healmes qu'il unt a or sartiz
> Tries lur espalles, tuz li bois reflambist
> Qui les veïst esleissier e saillir,
> De durs vassals li peüst sovenir.
> Idunc les mustret Viviëns Esturmi.
> (*Chanson de Guillaume* 232-40)

Thus it is clear that the effects created by tenses are entirely dependent upon the mood or tone which these tenses create and upon whether or not they can in any way be found to spatialize a particular scene.

II. Temporal Distortions

A number of factors may directly affect the chronology and pace of the text. The best general work to date on these problems is that of Gérard Genette found in his discussion of the structural study of narrative in *Figures III*.[9] Of interest to us are the categories Genette calls anachrony, anisochrony, and frequency.

Anachrony deals with the interjection of an analepsis ("flashback") or a prolepsis ("flashforward") into the primary narrative, that is, where an element of the *histoire* appears out of its normal place in the *récit*. Genette goes into some detail to specify all possible types of occurrences such as "homodiegetic external analepses" (episodes about the same character but all of which logically precede the starting point of the primary narrative), "heterodiegetic internal analepses" (episodes posterior to the starting point of the primary narrative and involving different characters or a story line different from the primary narrative), and so on. These distinctions, however, are really inconsequential with respect to the question of duration versus spatial time. What we observe for the most part in the old French epic is a situation where the *histoire* and the *récit* are coincident, but where this is not the case, any semblance of duration will be broken.

Given the fact that the future is relatively poorly defined in the epic and poorly represented in the tense system, it is no surprise that there are few prolepses here. Those which do occur are often found in the forms of dreams or visions. The prologues of the *Guillaume* (1-10) and the *Prise* (31-38) as well as the passage in the *Moniage* (96-99) where what is about to happen at Aniane is foretold are a few of the limited examples. Analepses tend to recount past events as means of citing "how things used to be and ought to be again" or as means of explaining how things came to be the way they are now. Examples include: Vivien's instructions to Girart to seek aid from Guillaume in the battle at Archamps by reminding him of his, Vivien's, past service to Guillaume (*Chanson de Guillaume* 635-89); Rainouart's story of his early life (*Chanson de Guillaume* 3507-48; *Aliscans* laisses CLXXXIVb-CLXXXIVc and vv. 4870-84); the story of Guillaume's dubbing of Vivien at Termes (*Chanson de Guillaume* 2001-05); a report of what has happened to Guillaume's men at Archamps (*Chanson de Guillaume* 2337-75 and 2510-51); the story of Mahomet's demise in the *Couronnement* (847-53); reminders of all Guillaume has done for Louis without apparent gratitude (*Charroi de Nîmes* 153-277); reference in the *Prise d'Orange* back to the events of the *Charroi* (13-16); Gillebert's story of Orange and his captivity (*Prise d'Orange* 184-282); Landri's story in the *Moniage Guillaume* (3311-68); Anseis's story of having tried to find Guillaume in Provence (*Moniage Guillaume* 5069-5111); and Bertran del Fossé's story of Guillaume's secret visit to Paris in the *Moniage Guillaume* (6415-62). There is another kind of anachrony as well in these epics, and that concerns the prayers that can interrupt the action. Vivien's prayer in the midst of the battle of Archamps (*Chanson de Guillaume* 800-37) is an analepsis recalling events from Biblical history, while at the same time exhorting aid, as are Guillaume's prayers in the *Prise d'Orange* (499-509 and 804-17). In such cases it is impossible for the listener to maintain any sense of temporal continuity or duration with what is taking place before him, and duration is thus broken as with any anachrony be it analepsis or prolepsis.[10]

Anisochrony is the situation obtained when there is an acceleration or deceleration of the *histoire* in relationship to the *récit*. Examples include expressions such as *n'i a plus demore* (*Aliscans* 1531), *n'a soing de l'atargier* (*Aliscans* 1549a), *Grant fu l'estors, longuement a dure* (*Aliscans* 5791), *de neient ne se targe* (*Couronnement de Louis* 252), *De ci qu'al tertre ne s'i volt atargier* (*Couronnement de Louis* 606). Assuming, again, that in the absence of elements which would destroy durational time we appreciate duration where *histoire* and *récit* are coincident, then anisochrony will itself destroy a sense of duration. It is all but impossible to find examples of decelerative anisochrony in the epic, that is, cases where the time of the *récit* is greater than the time of the *histoire*. Such procedures are more typical of modern literature, particularly where psychological or philosophical analysis is of importance. Proust is a good example. In early narrative, however, we are much more likely to find only TR (*récit*) = TH (*histoire*), or TH>TR, which is the case in which there is a conflation of events.

Actually there are several types of situations possible within the TH>TR group. One is that in which what might take days or even weeks to accomplish is related in one or two verses: *De ça Orenge ne voldrent arester* (*Aliscans* 7806) or *De ci en Brie n'arestent ne ne targent* (*Couronnement de Louis* 1449). What is accomplished "without delay" may be possible or it may not, but in any case the listener is made aware immediately of the rush of time. Related to this is an expression such as *De lor jornees ne sai que vos contasse* (*Couronnement* 1448) where the length of time it takes to do something is inconsequential (otherwise it would not be unknown), but where it is of great importance to stress that a quantity, probably a significant quantity, of time has passed. Finally, there can be situations where the poet will tell us exactly how much time passes during a particular event, such as the fifteen days Guillaume takes to gather troops and the three years he spends at Poitiers in the *Couronnement* (1999-2003), or the seven years Guillaume spends in Synagon's prison in the *Moniage* (3460). This last example is a particularly good one in terms of TH>TR for not only are we made aware of a long and specific period of time, but we also suddenly realize how much *histoire* has been conflated into relatively little *récit* in the Synagon episode. In any anisochrony, however, duration is broken and the listener suddenly becomes aware of the passage of time, of spatial time.

Finally, what Genette calls temporal frequency concerns the relations of repetition between *histoire* and *récit*. The poet may tell once what happens once; this is the basic narrative form of the epic. Or he may repeat an event *n* times, a technique which manifests itself as the epic *laisse similaire*.[11] The latter type of frequency is another factor in the destruction of duration, for as the listener hears a scene or event repeated, even in slightly different words with accents on different aspects of the event, he becomes aware of the cessation of the temporal flow and thus aware of time as a series of points laid out in space.

III. Formulas

Certain formulaic temporal expressions found in all of the Guillaume poems have the capacity to break duration by virtue of their reference to the passage of time or to specific moments in time. The following are representative;

—clers fu li jurz e bels fu li matins (*Chanson de Guillaume* 1730)
—quant l'albe pert (*Chanson de Guillaume* 2718)
—a tel hure (*Chanson de Guillaume* 2923)
—a iceste hure (*Chanson de Guillaume* 3002)
—Biaus fu li jors, li solaus raia cler (*Aliscans* 4601a)
—Biaus fu li jors et li solaus levés (*Aliscans* 4956)

—Biax fu li jors, miëdis fu passés (*Aliscans* 6649+1)
—un de cez jors (*Charroi de Nîmes* 76)
—jamés jor de sa vi (*Prise d'Orange* 1295)
—a icel tans (*Moniage Guillaume* 4682)

Either we become aware of a momentary break while time itself is appreciated, that is, where time seems to stop momentarily (e.g, *clers fu li jurz e bels fu li matins*), or we become aware of a point in time out of the durational flow (e.g., *a iceste hure* , or *quant l'albe pert*). Such expressions are similar to one we have already mentioned with respect to the anisochronic *De lor jornees ne vos sai aconter.* While both types of expressions are formulaic and both tend to create the same effect, the list cited above is different in that this group does not have any anisochronic function but rather focuses upon moments or periods of time separated out from what would otherwise be a durational flow.

IV. Isolated Temporal Markers

Related to the above formulaic expressions are a group of isolated words which also have the ability to spatialize the text from a temporal point of view.

In the following passage, nominal time references break any sense of duration by focusing upon specific times of the day as separated from other periods or by singling out such periods in the flow of events:

Tante jor fait son hauberc rooler,
Et son ceval tout de novel ferer
Et de grant jour sa provende doner;
Ensi le fait jusques a l'avesprer
(*Moniage* 5320-23)

Likewise a verse such as *La nuis fu bele et la lune luist cler* (*Moniage* 5349) has the same effect. The following also breaks up the day into spatial segments:

L'une moitié en ai anuit usé,
L'autre servoie le matin au disner:

> Ce vous donrai, se prendre le volés,
> Si ne m'avrai demain dont desjuner,
> Ains m'esterra jusc'au soir consieurrer.
> (*Moniage* 5785-89)

The conjunction *puis* may also have a spatializing effect in that it suggests that things are happening in series, that is to say that the poet has established a clear progression or sequence of events. This sequencing cannot fail to signal divided units of time even if it is only a question of two distinct events or periods. We find also that adverbial expressions such as *maintenant, isnelement, tost et delivrement* (*Prise* 1814), *tost et isnelement* (*Couronnement* 2643), *De France issimes il n'a mie lonc tens* (*Prise* 86), and *Dedenz Orenge ou ai grant piece esté* (*Prise* 159) draw attention to time either as in the case of an accelerated anisochrony or by defining, however vaguely, a particular span of time.

V. Appositional Mode

The appositional mode is another technique which can be used to establish or maintain duration, one which can be found as early as the literature of ancient Greece and Rome. Harry and Agathe Thornton describe this mode in *Time and Style: a psycholinguistic essay in Classical literature* where Homeric language is analyzed as presentation proceeding by way of succession rather than subordination and in which are found the two modes, linear and appositional. The appositional mode is that wherein an essential idea is given with details for ornament with emotional content then added in. The following passage describing Odysseus's arrival at Circe's abode is an example:

> I stood in the doorway of the goddess, the lovely-tressed one. There standing I shouted, and the goddess heard my cry, and she quickly coming out, the doors opened, the shining ones, and invited me in. And I followed, sad in my heart; and she seated me, leading me in, on a chair silver-nailed, beautiful, artfully wrought, and underneath there was a stool, for the feet!
> (*Odyssey* 10, 310ff.)

The Thorntons point out that the appositional mode has two distinctive features: (1) time as implied in this mode is not clearly or necessarily differentiated into past, present, and future, and any differentiation is rudimentary and partial; expectation spans but a minimum of the future, and the past is felt and experienced so vividly that it seems little removed from the present; (2) the temporal succession characteristic of the appositional mode is one of continual "return" to what was impulsively seized upon first, and this succession is determined by affect, that is by the positive feelings of delight and interest in the speaker and listener. Corollary to (1) they note that in this mode chronology is not necessarily followed, that the actual sequence of events is of no account. This is apparent in the passage reproduced above where it is apparent that a positive feeling-tone is the central concern, not the ordering of events.

The Thorntons show that the appositional style fits the mold of a qualitative or perceptual time-notion, not an abstract or conceptional one, which is what we find predominating in later literature and which has to do more with linear, and what we are calling spatial, time.

> What distinguishes appositional utterance is that it is an experience of a minimum of a future that is certainly to be expected and in part predetermined. As for the past, it is not strictly separated from the present as a past that has been and is no more, but is always close behind the present intensifying and illuminating it. One might go so far as to say that it is still part and parcel of the present as immediately experienced by narrator and listener. Considerable affective or emotional intensity is also achieved through the process of "reviving" memory images from their evanescence. (86)

They conclude that:

> time, in the early phase of classical thought, is not yet an abstract frame of reference within which events take place at definable points, but it is so closely tied to events that, apart from them, it does not appear to exist. Further, time is not devoid of quality, but it takes its "coloring" or "feel" from the events to which it belongs. This time notion is in fact concrete and qualitative. (119)

The Thorntons are really talking about *duration*. In their view the affective aspect accords with the intensely emotional nature of man in the Homeric epics. Perhaps it is not surprising, therefore, given the often highly emotional nature of the Old French epics, that the appositional mode should occasionally be found there as well.

The following is typical of the kind of appositional style that can be found in the Guillaume epics:

> Lunsdi al vespre.
> Li Sarazin de Saraguce terre
> Cent mile furent de cela pute geste;
> N'i out celui de blanc halberc ne's veste,
> De Saraguce verz healmes en lur testes,
> D'or les fruntels e les flurs e les esses,
> Espees ceintes, les branz burniz vers terre;
> Les bons escuz tindrent as maneveles,
> Espiez trenchanz e darz en lur poinz destres,
> Chevals coranz d'Arabe suz lur seles.
> Cil fors issirent el sable, en la gravele;
> Si i purpristrent defors certeine terre.
> Cunte Tedbald moürent cil grant guere:
> Pur ço orrez doleruse novele.
> (*Guillaume* 218-31)

This passage is clearly designed to elicit a certain affective response from the listener, and it is obvious also that the ordering of events is inconsequential given that the description of the Saracens on their horses is presented before we are told that they have emerged onto the beach from their ships. While we may not have here the *positive* feeling tone the Thorntons describe in the Homeric epics, it is the establishment of an affective state that is important, for this will help to create duration and ultimately generate a particular response from the audience that will be within the desired ethical stance of the epic.

Such examples are not frequent enough in the epics to be given major credit for the establishment of duration, but their occurrence has a tendency to further or to restore duration established by other means. Related to the appositional mode as we have described it are occasions where, although there is no play with the ordering of events, the gradual addition of detail to a scene creates a particular tone to the text and assists the listener in experiencing a sense of duration in the absence of any temporal indicators. There are many such cases already well known as epic description.

The foregoing leads us to what may be called the "emotional value" of epic temporality. Put simply, this means that the past lives in the present because it has value for the present and because it is capable of generating actions or satisfying the exigencies of an ethical system. There is no real historical detachment in the Old French epic. That is, what is narrated is not objective fact or even what the poet or audience thinks the past events to be. What is told about is rather what *is* or what will satisfy contemporary ethical constructs. What is told, once again, is a myth, and myths are not of the past but of the present or perhaps the present as indistinguishable from the past. The recitation of the myth, the ritual expression of it, revivifies the past and makes of it the present with a heavy emphasis upon the affective or emotional side of man as clearly distinguished from the cognitive or rational side. This is not to say that there is no "truth" to the epic; we are simply not concerned here with empirically verifiable truth. Yet, there is nothing truer to the spirit of man than the epic myth. Thus, the past and present remain inexorably fused and indistinguishable from one another during the performance of the text. The significance this has for us is that the overall temporal framework in which the epic is composed is one in which duration, or an undivided temporal unity, is established with previous recitations of text as well as with the events which gave rise to the text itself. In other words, nonspatial or durational temporality is the basis upon which the poem is narrated. Whatever breaks the sense of duration here must do so for specific reasons.[12]

The durational style of the epic, with its readily apparent affective aspect, is due primarily to the careful orchestration of tenses, an occasional use of the appositional mode, and the creation of a dramatic, emotional tone. Duration, however, can also be destroyed through tense usage, as well as by means of temporal distortions, formulas, and the use of isolated temporal markers. The shifting between duration (or nonspatial time) and spatial time is important, for the result of the shift between spatial and nonspatial temporality has implications for the listener's response to the text.

During duration, the listener is drawn into the text and made a part of the ethical world of the epic by virtue of the affective aspect of duration and the flow of events which he does not spatialize. This is important, for it allows the listener the opportunity to become one with the situation, to grasp it, apprehend it, and to associate with it. It is at these moments that the listener participates most actively in the timeless myth; duration is thus an integral, if not basic, element of the myth as established by the "petit cycle." When duration is broken and time is spatialized, however, the listener is effectively held at a distance from the action of the poem by virtue of becoming conscious of the spatial nature of time or of events as set out as points in space.

As the text becomes spatialized the listener is set at a distance from it and he takes on more the role of the observer. It is important for the poet to be able to spatialize the text, for it allows him to guarantee a certain perspective on the part of the listener, particularly if he, the poet, is to maintain the didactic function of the epic. Beyond that, however, spatial time is significant because it is tied to the overall structure of the epic. While we maintain that epic temporality is essentially durational but with regular disruptions of spatial time, we cannot ignore the fact of the highly spatial nature of this poetry, and it is to that subject that we now turn.

Chapter Five

Space

OLD FRENCH EPIC POETRY APPEARS to defy any critical attempts at precision with regard to space just as it does to time: the barren stage of epic scenery, the apparent lack of "realism" (at least in our terms), and the frequent distortion of actual topography and geography often create a strange panorama. The aspect of space, however, is perhaps the most important in the Guillaume epics for it is that which unifies not only individual poems but the total image of Guillaume as derived from the collection. Together with time it is also responsible for the mythic nature of this poetry.

Literary spatiality is many things. It can mean the pictorial imagery projected by means of verbal portraits, the narrative structure created by repetition and analogy (e.g., "ring structure"), the context or field of rhetorical figures, the social or cultural space represented in the text, or the textual space in which text and interpreter interact and in which both the generation of the text and the process of "reading" it are related.[1]

Space is not a subject which has always been thought to be an integral element of literary art, although it has certainly been studied more extensively recently. Lessing's famous essay, *Laocoon*, is well known as an attempt to make generic distinctions between the verbal and plastic arts, and it is there that he notes that literature is essentially a temporal art while the plastic arts are primarily spatial. The reason appears obvious: literary narrative is unfolded over time while painting or sculpture are apprehended in a moment of time as complete works. Few will argue today that literature is primarily temporal in nature, although Lessing, for example, no doubt never intended to exclude spatiality totally from considerations of literature.

Nevertheless, many literary works support Lessing's views and are in fact constructed within a clear temporal framework while many others seems just as clearly devoid of a temporal nature and can be said to exist extra-temporally, or spatially. In the latter case, we are talking about myth, a fact which will be demonstrated in the course of this chapter.

Phenomenologically speaking literary texts are as spatial as they are temporal if not more so. It has nonetheless taken writers such as Georges Poulet (*La distance intérieur*), Gaston Bachelard (*La poétique de l' espace*), Maurice Blanchot (*L'espace littéraire*), and Gérard Genette (essays in *Figures I, II, III*) to name some of the more prominent, to permit us to appreciate this fact. Our apprehension of the substance of the text may be the result of a temporal process, of accretions of bits of information over time, a time which very often approximates the experience of human time, but our conception of this textual substance most often occupies a certain measure of mental space. Now this measure of mental space is never fixed, nor can it in fact ever be "measured" because it is constantly in a state of change, modification, or flux due to the addition of new bits of information or due to our revision of how we see this substance. Besides, there are no limits against which we can measure such a conception, for our literary mental space is limited only by our imagination and the creative ability of the poet. This space, which is generated and given shape and form by the process of the text, and which may be called our "image" of its textual substance, may not only defy time by virtue of its extra-temporal nature, but it ultimately leaves us with a more vivid picture of the text than anything temporality could offer us. Indeed, it is even difficult to discuss a literary text without recourse to such terms as "image" and "picture," so strong is our tendency to establish some sort of framework to what we perceive. The very process of description—and we shall hazard to say that no literary text can exist without embodying description of some kind—demands, teases us into creating an image in our minds. It is a perfectly natural response to the unknown or to the unfamiliar, for what can be delimited and defined, given shape and form, suddenly loses its unfamiliarity or even fearsomeness. What motivates the artist *qua* artist is to define the human experience. The architect, the sculptor, and the painter concern themselves with this visually as means of giving shape and form to their conceptions of man in relationship to his world; the poet using words likewise wills form and shape to his conceptions, but instead of projecting them outward he projects them inward onto our consciousness where we do the final arranging, the final giving of shape and form to the image of the text. Literary art may be more flexible than the plastic or visual arts by allowing greater participation in the artistic process, but it is no less spatial from a generic point of view. In point of fact it may be said to be more so given the demands toward spatialization placed upon the interpreter.

The process of internalizing the text, of participating in the creation or the spatialization of it, may be a natural part of the literary experience, but it may also be particularly characteristic of the medieval experience. In a discussion of the plastic arts, Marshall McLuhan and Harley Parker state that:

> The Renaissance was unconsciously engaged in creating a pervasive visual space that was uniform, continuous and connected, but the Middle Ages had had a very different kind of space as its psychic and social environment. One of the reasons for this was the "idea" behind Medieval representation. It was the idea rather than the psychological narrative connectives between figures that was central to Medieval communication. There was no need for a rational or continuous space in which the figures could find psychological interaction. (*Through the Vanishing Point* 12)

While the "vanishing point" in Renaissance art is in the painting such that the spectator sees the space of the painting as continuous with his own, the vanishing point in medieval art is in the mind of the interpreter such that the work is read out in terms of the communicated idea. Such factors as perspective, foreshortening, modeling, chiaroscuro, and all those elements normally associated with later Renaissance and "naturalistic" forms of art may thus be absent from medieval art with no apparent consequence. What matters is not what is seen on the surface of the art object itself, but rather how the elements of that art object will be decoded and interpreted in the mind of the beholder. This is a given today.

The process of internalization is not limited to the beholder; the artist places himself inside the work as well. Boris Uspensky has remarked that "Since the Renaissance the position of the artist in European fine arts as regards the picture has been, generally speaking, external; in Ancient and Medieval painting, however, the artist located himself inside the work, picturing the world around him; that is, his position was not alienated, external, but internal as regards the picture" ("Structural Isomorphism of Verbal and Visual Art" 11-12). He goes on to point out that the internal source of light often seen in the center of a medieval picture turning into shadow at the periphery corresponds to the internal position of the observer/artist inside the picture. The manipulation of space in medieval art is therefore every bit as important as it may be in later forms of art. We think that in some ways it may be even more important because of the efforts at internalizing on the part of both creator and interpreter. Not only does it appear that the artist puts himself into the art object as a way of picturing the world around him, but it may be suggested that this may have filled a psychological need to define the space of his world and his place in it, especially as this relates to epic poetry. The interpreter of the poem in turn is afforded the opportunity to become part of the textual space of the poem and to participate in the process of spatializing the epic world. This can be a very useful, even comforting, experience for someone participating in what in reality is a very chaotic world.

There is sufficient, if not to say abundant, evidence that the Old French epic manifests not only a concern for spatiality but manifests it as a way of dealing with an external world in chaos, that is to say as an opportunity for the interpreter to come to terms with his world on his own terms. It is with regard to spatiality that the listener of epic poetry finally is able to take something from his experience with the text, to bridge that gap between the text and himself, and to participate in the myth. An examination of the spatial framework of this poetry, the manipulation of space internal to the texts, and the relationship between the space of the text and the interpreter bears this out.

Spatial Framework

The general spatial framework of these epics may be conceived of as two broad areas: "concrete," or visual spatiality resulting from physical descriptions, landscaping, geography, etc.; and, "abstract" spatiality, or that which results from literary structure such as repetition and analogy.

The visual imagery resulting from physical description is dependant upon the semiosis discussed in chapter three. Not only is the simple physical picture that we obtain of Guillaume, Rainouart, and others a result of the interplay of semes and sememes concerning these figures, but those semes and sememes which concern their more abstract and psychological qualities also combine to generate the mythemes of individual personnages. We recognize, of course, that the semiosis of particular events in which a given personnage participates also helps to create a visual, physical picture of the individual, although this is never a true photographic image of any epic figure. While we may know that Charlemagne has a long, flowing, white beard, or that Guillaume has a distinctive nose, and while we may have some idea of the physical beauty of Orable, we never get beyond the archetypal image of such prominent figures slightly modified by these distinctive traits. Yet at the point at which we begin to obtain a visual image of a figure, however imperfectly described, our own imagination begins modeling the rough space provided us by the poet by means of his description. In this way the process of spatial definition begins; and to a large extent it is dependent upon us, not the poet. The sketchiness of epic description effectively creates a spatial void which demands definition, and as we will see, the urge towards spatial definition is a major function of the epic.

The poet has at his disposal other types of description which ultimately serve to give us a spatial picture of the action. Reference to a particular setting—a castle, a room, *Terre Certeine*, names of cities or regions—offers us the possibility of localization and framing.[2] As Curtius and Calin have shown, the epic setting is highly stylized and sparse as well as inaccurate. The inaccuracy, however, is inconsequential, for what is important are the symbolic overtones, the archetypal loci which result from classic epic scenery.[3] The use of physical space is clearly intended to do more than simply offer a visual picture of the setting and action of the epic even if it must do that first.

The death of Vivien by the *duit troblé* in the *Guillaume* conveys a moving sense of agony, of loneliness, and of emptiness. Guillaume's imprisonment in Synagon's *chartre* in the *Moniage* projects a similar sense of loneliness and agony as well as despair and hopelessness. In these cases it is not only their plaintive attitudes but their silences and the limited yet clear descriptions of the harsh settings in which they are found that create a sense of space, in the one case vacuous, in the other confining.

Beyond such emotive qualities of physical description there may also be more obvious metaphorical aspects. The casting of Gui d'Allemagne into the Tiber (*Couronnement*) or the Saracens into the Seine (*Moniage*) serves to underscore the moral tone carried by Guillaume's actions. Likewise the hero's ability to transform the city from pagan to

Christian (*Prise*) stands as a clear symbol of the rightness and power of the side of God. As Eugene Vance has shown with respect to the *Roland*, spatial relationships can be profound metaphors for the structure of man's moral life ("Spatial Structure in the *Chanson de Roland*"). The city of Orange stands as the physical and moral center of the poem and as such becomes the focus not only for the action of the poem but for its underlying meaning as well.[4]

The foregoing techniques are certainly not new to the Old French epic; they follow in an impressive tradition dating back to the ancient writers of Greece and Rome. Theodore M. Andersson, in an excellent study of epic scene design extending from the classical period into the Middle Ages, shows how the Homeric epic is not only capable of making action ebb and flow in space but how it also excels in giving shape to experience for the purpose of illuminating the inner world. As for the Virgilian epic, he determines the following to be characteristic of its spatial design:

> the outlining of a scene before it is narrated, the view from alternating distances, visualization through the use of various lines and shapes, animation through sight, sound, and motion, the abundant use of contrast, revelation in the eye of a beholder, and the application of complementary perspective. To this must be added the enriching of almost every scene, beyond the purely pictorial qualities, with emotional and symbolic meanings.
> (*Early Epic Scenery* 75)

While some of these characteristics of Virgil are not to be found in the twelfth-century epic, vestiges of many of them are. Andersson makes the case that Virgilian style can be seen reflected in ninth-century Latin poems such as *Karolus Magnus et Leo Papa*, *In Honorem Hludowici*, and *Waltharius*. *Beowulf* may have undergone Virgilian influence as well. None of this affirms the same for the later vernacular epics—nor does it matter greatly one way or other, perhaps—but there is certainly room to suspect the classical poets of sharing their style with those of the twelfth century, and if the latter lack the elaboration or flair of their models, this may say more about the unique skills of the ancient epic poets and the newly developing skills of later poets awakening to newer needs of a different time than anything else.

The overriding spatial impression of the medieval epic which results from the interplay of physical description, localization, and topography is still what we have long called the "tableau." The still-frame technique reminds us of a polychrome on wood painting, a near frozen-action shot which has the tendency to magnify its own image until it takes on mythic proportions. This is an absolutely essential fact of the epic if it is to project not only a mythic image to be admired and emulated but also a transcendent or immanent sign essential to the correct reading of the message of the text and the proper motivation of the listener. The listener is being asked not just to hear but to act, and the text is that medium or vehicle which brings him into contact with the message or myth that the society at large is attempting to articulate. Guillaume and Rainouart are not simply admirable heroes. They are the incarnation of a living spirit, of a mode of existence, of a means of response to the external and internal world of time. The monumental images which they project are thus all-important and they must take on a certain status in order to be able to embody and communicate the desired message.[5] It is important, however, to realize that none of this is in any way dependant upon realism in description, topography, or the like. What matters is the image or sign which is shaped and formed in the mind of the interpreter through the sparsity of detail and because of it. Jean-Charles Payen reminds us that "...le décor épique fait généralement fi de la perspective et concentre les évènements dans l'espace et le temps.... C'est pourquoi le lieu des exploits épiques est si indéfini" ("Le *Charroi de Nîmes,* comédie épique?" 900). It must be indefinite if the active mental participation of the listener is to be engaged. Thus we once again affirm verticality over horizontality in the epic.[6]

Abstract epic spatiality refers to that type of space created at one remove from the purely pictorial created by means of structural repetition and analogy. This is a spatial characteristic which serves to tie the text together, to unify it into a literary whole. It may be composed of foreshadowing of events, of flashbacks, of events in series recalling one another, or of simple repetition or recall of the same event.

The *Couronnement* is a good example of simple structural repetition in that Guillaume proceeds through a predictable pattern of activities, emerging from a rest phase to eliminate a threat to society and subsequently returning to a peaceful locus once he has completed the work phase of a cycle. Each Branch stands as an echo of the ones preceding and following it; had one cared to do so, the *Couronnement* could presumably have been carried on indefinitely through a number of Branches like the *Roman de Renart.* The Branches not only echo one another but also cause the listener to reflect upon what he has already heard and to anticipate what is to come. In this way a sense of the whole of the text as well as the image and myth of Guillaume is appreciated, and it is done so extra-temporally or spatially. Likewise the adventures of Guillaume in the *Moniage* can be seen as a series of analogous events. His clearing the desert of Provence of vermin and robbers echoes, metaphorically, his cleansing the monastery at Aniane of an ungodly prior. This then looks forward to this periodic cleaning of the *chartre* at Synagon's palace and the tearing up of weeds in his garden. Symbolically he is concerned with a moral act more than a purely feudal one, and each of these acts reinforces itself in the reflection of the others. The proper reading of the text is thus done both retrogressively as well as progressively, but the ultimate effect is less a temporal process than it is the development of a spatial, textual mosaic.[7]

The most striking type of spatial structure is undoubtedly the ring as manifested in "ring composition."[8] This is a means of developing an oral narrative in an ABCDCBA fashion wherein the first elemental corresponds to the last, the second to the next to last, and so on, usually with a "kernel" element at the midpoint of the narrative where a highly significant event takes place that is central to the entire text. The series can theoretically be carried out indefinitely with the result that an ever-expanding set of concentric rings develops.

In "Ring Composition in *La Chanson de Roland* and *La Chançun de Willame*," John D. Niles demonstrates how the *Guillaume* can be seen as neatly divided into the three major battles, preceded by the setting which will lead into the first battle at Archamps and followed at the end by the reconciliation of Guillaume and Rainouart and the banquet scene. At the very center is found the slaying of Deramed and the temporary revival of Vivien which Niles describes as a "breakthrough from the everyday human world to an 'other' world of death and more than human power" (12). Niles reminds us that the same phenomonen occurs in the *Roland* where the sun stops in mid-sky while Marsile's army is drowned; in *Beowulf* where Grendel's dam is slain; and in the *Odyssey* where the hero visits the world of the dead to speak with the shade of Teiresias. The question is then whether or not ring composition can be found in the other Guillaume poems we are considering.

The answer is that with some effort a series of rings can be established for the *Aliscans* which is not surprising since it is another version of the story related in the *Chanson de Guillaume*. The ring structure of the *Aliscans* is not nearly as neat as in the earlier poem. It is difficult to find corresponding events of parallel significance in the latter part of the poem as in the first, although there are echoing events such as the first great battle at Archamps presided over by Guillaume, the last one presided over primarily by Rainouart, and Guillaume and Rainouart's first arrival at Orange, which is later echoed by their joint and victorious reentry into the city. There is even a kind of kernel episode near the middle of the poem where there is a reference to the dying Vivien and the *fontaine* (4194-96), although the actual episode referred to occurs early in the poem (695). There is no central kernel episode like that found in the *Chanson de Guillaume*, the *Roland*, or *Beowulf*.

The *Couronnement, Charroi, Prise,* and *Moniage* do not manifest any appreciable ring structure of the kind found in these other poems. While again, there are certainly events which tend to echo one another, the precise structure of ring composition is not present. This in no way devalues the poems, however, for their spatial structure is simply dependent upon other factors, and we would say that the important element in the abstract spatial structure of them is what we have just referred to as echoing.

We have already indicated that in the *Couronnement* Guillaume's actions answer or forecast what he does in other Branches. In the *Charroi* we find a thematic echoing where Guillaume's refusal early on to break up the lands of other Franks is later answered by his return, intact, of the barrels and carts used in the conquest of Nîmes. Guillaume will not sacrifice lands or goods of friends or peers for his own gain. In the *Prise* we find a constant coming and going from Orange with the liberation of the city coming both from within and from outside its walls, the very penetrable nature of the city announcing Guillaume's ultimate liberation despite his temporary captivity. In the *Moniage*, we find Guillaume as the would-be postulant who would unwittingly destroy Aniane because of his voracious appetite later answered by the cenobite who is the perfect steward of his environment. Each of these types of echoing, together with the perennial series of battles in which Guillaume engages, creates a framework just as strong as that provided by ring composition, and in all cases the result of these kinds of structuring is a spatial framework in which the drama of the poem can be played out, a stage or domain given over to this epic world. Let us now look at another way in which the poet can manipulate space within the text as a means of defining this world.

Space Modulation

Among other concerns, a major preoccupation of the Old French epic is the getting and holding of land. What is interesting about this concern in the Guillaume Cycle is what might be called a "space modulation phenomenon" consisting of an interplay between relatively small, contained spaces or specific loci contrasted with vast, undefined or limitless spaces. This phenomenon is particularly striking in the *Chanson de Guillaume*. We begin our study of it there.

The stark polarity between relatively defined and undefined areas of space is fitting in the binary world of the epic. We read that Vivien drinks from a *duit* and dies by a *tertre*, that Guillaume moves suddenly from one city to another, and that he addresses his barons in a *bone sale*. In contrast we read that the Saracens come from across the sea, that Archamps is *estrange cuntree*, and that Guillaume will flee into the void if he thinks he has disgraced his people—all suggesting vast, undefined space. In between there is nothing; no spatial gradient connecting these polar opposites, no middle ground nor spatial context, no perspective.

Most references to defined or undefined spaces in the epic are diffuse and seem to fall into no recognizable pattern. But among the many references to space (which run literally into the hundreds in any given poem) a rhythm is established within four unique pairs or types of references, that is situations in which the polar spatial opposites are mentioned. Type I concerns a situation in which a character has a view out over an expanse of space contrasting with his position in a relatively small, defined space. In the *Guillaume*, for example, when Tedbald arises in the morning, still groggy from a night of revelry, he

> Devers le vent ouvrit une fenestre,
> Mirat le ciel ne pot mirer la terre:
> Vit la coverte de broines e de helmes,
> (*Guillaume* 100-03)

Here we find Tedbald in a closely, clearly defined space, presumably that of his *chambre*, and contrasted with that space a seemingly limitless one extending as far as the eye can see for *ne pot mirer la terre*. A similar situation is found as Vivien surveys the field at Archamps:

> Viviëns garde par mi une champaigne,
> Devant ses oilz vit la fiere compaigne,
> Del mielz de France pur grant bataille faire.
> Mulz en vit d'els gisir en cele place.
> (*Guillaume* 473-76)

Likewise we find Guibourc at the palace at Barcelona awaiting Guillaume's return from battle while tending to the care and feeding of more troops,

> Dunc s'apuiad a un marbrin piler
> Par la fenestre prist fors a esgarder,
> E vit Guillelme par un tertre avaler,
> Un home mort devant lui aporter.
> (*Guillaume* 1240-43)

In each case the person is in an explicitly named or implied closed space casting a look out over a wide, undefined space. It is as if the poet is offering to the individual, or to us, the opportunity to gain perspective, to assess one's circumstances, or to withdraw from a tense situation. This offers a visual command of a large area of space, generally the area which the Franks are attempting to command physically.

Type II paired space involves travel over a vast area from point A to point B. Examples include Vivien's sending Girard from Archamps to Barcelona to seek Guillaume's help (633-34, 696-741), Guillaume's return to Barcelona after a battle at Bordeaux (933-36), and the latter's trip from Barcelona to Archamps (1083-93). In such cases the person involved has the opportunity to command a large, undefined space while moving between two seemingly specific locations. The journey between the two covers an area so poorly defined it may not be described at all, but that in itself evokes questions about it and about the abrupt shift between tableaux. Perhaps the intervening area between points A and B is of no importance to the poet who limits himself to occasional topographical descriptions of such areas as seen in Girard's returns to Barcelona. I think, however, that the function of such contrasts may be to make the defined areas stand out all the more.

Type III paired space concerns a person's entry into or exit from a vast, undefined space contrasted with his situation in a small defined space. Here are included such cases as Deramed's emergence from the sea to seize Archamps (38, 149), and the Saracens' flight from Archamps to their ships on the sea—*Acuillent fuie devers l'eve de mer/Si entrent tost es barges e es nefs* (1701-02). The Saracens here are obviously in search of containment and protection from the Franks, but from the intended listener's point of view they are bound for the void. In both G1 and G2 the Saracens come from *terra incognita*, from across the sea. In fact, at one point near the end of the poem we hear:

> Diënt paien: "Mult fames grant folie,
> K'a cest diäble nus laissum ci oscire.
> Fuium nus ent en mer, en cel abisme,
> La u noz barges sunt rengées e mises!"
> (*Guillaume* 3334-37)

Finally, there is a fourth type of paired spatial expressions which we might label "social space" (Type IV). This concerns social voids or the absence of necessary persons in important situations and corresponding references to finite social situations where a critical individual is integrated into the society and thereby completes it or defines it as whole. In G1 all examples of this type of space occur before Guillaume's first battle at Archamps and concern his obvious absence, which has created a void in this warrior society. Says Vivien:

> Jo ai oï Looïs u Guillelme;
> S'il sunt venu, l'esturs ne durra gueres."
> (*Guillaume* 453-54)

Or we read later that:

> Mar fut li chans senz le cunte Guillelme.
> (*Guillaume* 472)

In contrast there is the obvious implication that things would all be put right were Guillaume at hand. It becomes clear then that Guillaume is needed to define his society or to complete it by filling a void.

The foregoing examples of a particular concern for space have all, save for one case, been taken from G1. Some sort of paired reference to space, defined and undefined, occurs about every thirty verses in this part, while an apparent indiscriminate use of an unpaired reference occurs approximately every ten verses. An explanation for this frequency may be found in G2.

Some interesting observations should first be made about the second half of the poem. Paired references occur every forty-eight verses, unpaired every eight. This slight difference can certainly be attributed to different redactors. Frappier has observed, moreover, that "Le site de l'Archamp perd toute précision concrète dans G2, dont le poète, tout occupé à rendre l'action dans son mouvement et dans ce qu'elle a d'immédiat ne le voit jamais encadrée dans le paysage" (*Les chansons de geste du cycle de Guillaume d'Orange*, I, 203-04). Perhaps the poet, concerned with particular thematic intentions, did not need to be more specific about geography and topography, and after all, the listener is by now familiar with the site. Curiously, G2 has proportionately many fewer examples of Types I and III spatial pairs with three and six examples respectively while G1 contains eleven and seventeen respectively.[9] These differences may again be attributable to different redactors, but there is yet perhaps an even better explanation. The major difference between the content of G1 and G2 is Rainouart's presence in the latter. He is significant because he spells success for the Franks by finally securing their land for them, and he is closely related to the problem of finite and infinite space.

As G1 opens we learn that Deramed has arrived from across the sea and that a group of Franks has been taken prisoner. This evokes the void motif even with respect to the prisoners who are now in unknown territory. The Franks go to battle at Archamps, but we learn that although this is spoken of as a specific place (and may even be better described topographically than Rencesvals—see Frappier's comment on this in *Les chansons de geste...*, I, 171-72), it is also spoken of as *terra incognita* for Vivien commands Girard to bring Guiot along to help him in *estrange cuntree* (682). As Girard reaches Barcelona, Guillaume has returned to the palace after a battle at Bordeaux. He gathers troops in his *sale* (contained space), and sets out for the *estrange cuntree* as if to secure or define it for his own. He fails at first, returns to the confines of the palace, sets out again for Archamps, and succeeds this time with Gui's help. These cycles of action, Guillaume's alternating between defined and undefined space and the paired reference to space discussed above stand out in the listener's mental image of the poem. The final laisses of G1 find Guillaume racing around the battlefield on foot and horseback, securing the area, and defining it as his own. Although this territory was thought of as Frankish all along (Vivien even refers to it as *sa tere*, 495), a redactor has added G2 in spite of agreeing that *ore out vencu sa bataille Willame* (1980).[10] G2 goes on to make the point even more strongly that the capture and definition of land as one's own is a central concern.

Here we find familiar cycles of action of paired spatial references. Guillaume returns to the defined space of the palace where he refreshes in the comfort of his *bone sale*. This is an interesting passage, for the *sale* is where he is accustomed to finding his *grant barnage*, that is, his feudal society. Today, however, he bemoans the fact that the *sale*, the society, is falling apart because of the events at Archamps. His defined space is threatened. With that he then heads for Louis's court and finds help in that *sale* where an entire feudal society is gathered:

> En la sale out tels quinze chevaliers:
> Freres e uncles, parenz, cosins e nies,
> (*Guillaume* 2538-39)

The *sale* is where we expect to find a complete feudal society; it is defined space. Guillaume gathers an army, returns again to the palace at Orange, and sets out again for the *estrange cuntree*, this time with Rainouart. As these alternations between defined and undefined space continue, so do those paired references already discussed.

Rainouart now begins to take on significance as a spatial metaphor embodying the characteristics of both clearly defined and vast or undefined space, for he has emerged from the void, the Saracen world, and he is the efficient cause of the Franks' success which results in a clearly defined, unified Frankish world. It is he who effectively drives the Saracens back into the *abisme* and frees the captive Christians from the "void" of the Saracen ships. In so doing he earns a true place in his adoptive society. When he then threatens to return again to the *estrange cuntree* from whence he came, having been snubbed by Guillaume, the Franks must bring him back to guarantee the unity and wholeness of their world. They can now no more let him part than Guibourc could have let Guillaume disappear to the *estrange cuntree* of *Saint Michel al peril de la mer* (2414-15).

Rainouart had spent seven years as a kitchen knave; he is now baptised in his eighth year in Christian lands, both the act of baptism and the number eight having significance as symbols of completion or wholeness. As he becomes complete, so does his adoptive society. He has moved from the symbolic void of the Saracen world to a clearly defined Christian world while eliminating all symbols of undefined space (Saracens) from

Archamps. He, like Guillaume at the end of G1, races around the battlefield, chasing out the enemy and defining the territory as his own.

In an article entitled "Guillaume, Vivien, et Rainouart. Le souillé et le pur," Alfred Adler traces Rainouart's development from an *impur* character to a *pur* one where he earns a place in Frankish society. Adler bases his theory upon a dialectic of concrete elements, "une logique de qualité sensibles" taken from studies by Lévi-Strauss ("le cru et le cuit," "le frais et le pourri," etc.) which he believes may help explain medieval thought. To this may be added the dialectic of polar space. It is not one that involves a true Hegelian dialectical relationship, however. Rainouart, the spatial metaphor, unlike any other individual in the poem, represents a synthesis encompassing both defined and undefined space only in a limited sense because he ultimately stands only for the affirmation of the thesis, clearly defined space; he eliminates the antithesis completely. He fills a void found earlier in the society, and he defines the *estrange cuntree* of Archamps as solely Frankish. He brings the pendulum of the poem to rest on the positive pole of defined space, never really resolving the polar situation or creating a new synthesis out of it.

What happens in the *Chanson de Guillaume* with respect to polar spatial references is not unique although there is no Rainouart to serve as a convenient spatial metaphor in every poem in the Cycle. No matter. As the standard bearer of the collection it sets the tone for what follows, for in every poem space is modulated as a means of coming to terms with a hostile world.

The *Aliscans* exhibits the four types of paired spatial references found in the *Chanson de Guillaume* but with some unique twists to reinforce the metaphorical value of Rainouart. The fact that Rainouart does battle at Archamps with his brother, Walegrape, who is from the *mer betee*, underscores the need to define his sphere of influence. This is supported also by the encounter with his cousin, Baudus, who, once defeated, promises the fealty of the Saracens and who subsequently hastens off to the void for the purpose of bringing them back into the fold at the palace. The episode of the bean field, too, emphasizes the need to clearly define the spatial domain of the Franks, for a ravaged field turned into a wasteland, and occupied by elements of the void, is hardly acceptable in the unified whole toward which he is working. Finally, Rainouart is given Tortelose and Porpaillart as fiefs, cities by the sea, and it is clear that he is there to guard against invasion from abroad. He is now the consummate symbol of clearly defined, unified space, the protector against the threat of the undefined.

The figure of Rainouart is missing from the other four poems we are considering, but Guillaume is more than up to the task of going it alone in terms of spatial definition. The five Branches of the *Couronnement* take him across the face of the Empire including two visits to Rome and a year-long campaign in northern France.[11] The four types of paired spatial references are again at work here although Types I, II and IV appear to dominate.

In both the *Charroi* and the *Prise*, Type IV takes a back seat to the first three types. The barrel ruse is turned into an effective metaphor for well-defined, contained space which "spills over" to limit and define what previously was wild, undefined territory despite the fact that Nîmes is a closed city; it becomes defined in Frankish terms. The *Prise*, on the other hand, manifests a rather inverse process where the unacceptable void that is Orange is given definition from within by Guillaume, the captive, not by a conquering hero external to this space.

The *Moniage* then brings the process of spatial definition to its logical conclusion. Once again Guillaume sets out on a series of adventures, unwittingly this time, and once again he is responsible for the wholeness of the realm. He even has to eliminate a threat to the well-being of Aniane, that is the prior himself. Types I-IV of paired space occur again in the *Moniage* with a return to importance of Type IV which serves as an effective cause of his being called out of retirement in the Ysoré episode. By the time he is through, Guillaume has eliminated a threat to Aniane, giants and robbers in Provence, Synagon, Ysoré, and the bridge-devil. In so doing he defines all the territory in question as part of a wholly unified, Frankish/Christian domain. Throughout the Cycle it has been the subtle interplay of clearly defined and vast, undefined spatial images which have moved toward the final resolution seen in the *Moniage*. In all cases, any suggestions of unclearly defined, void, or hostile space must be eliminated. Uniquivocal spatial definition is of the utmost importance to the epic text.

Two results grow out of the interplay of polar spatial images just discussed. The first is the obvious definition of what is Frankish/Christian by means of military exploits. The second is the definition of the socio-cultural characteristics of the epic. It is not sufficient just to obtain and hold land; the way in which it is obtained and later held is of equal importance. In short, the feudal ethic comes into play such that it becomes clear to the listener of the text that the only space which receives clear definition is also feudal.[12] Both Guillaume and Rainouart operate according to feudal principles of order, discipline, and law. That which they obtain is done so through work, law, or the granting of fiefs, but only insofar as none of these principles is in violation of any one of the others according to feudal custom. Thus, Guillaume is quite simply unable to accept lands in the *Charroi* which the king would grant him upon the decease of their current holders and where legal descendants or guardians are waiting to be responsible for those lands. The feudal ethos appears to be very much alive in the Guillaume epics, so much so that Rainouart goes to great lengths in the *Chanson de Guillaume* and *Aliscans* to prove himself a worthy member of such a society by observing feudal ethics and customs and to ensure that liars or pretenders are exposed and eliminated from the society of the *Moniage*. In effect, the ethical world of Guillaume is one pole of a binary system consisting of the feudal ethos on the one hand, and one of chaos, lawlessness, and disgrace on the other. How, indeed, can the Saracen world be of any account when its spiritual leader has been devoured by swine! (*Couronnement* 845-53). There is an inner circle of acceptable values and within that space lies what we have been talking about. All that is external to it is unacceptable. It is the inner, sociocultural space of acceptability where the epic resides and of which the epic narrative is the process of definition.

The following diagram is a simple expression of the acceptable and unacceptable spaces of the epic:

Figure III

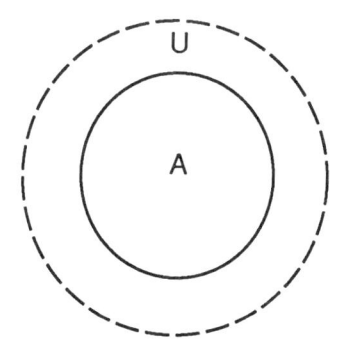

A represents the (ultimately) clearly defined cultural space of the Frankish world while U represents the unacceptable and unclearly defined space of the enemy world, the void, the *estrange cuntree*. A is delimited by a solid line to show that it is clearly defined, whole, complete—at least in theory, for it certainly will be at the conclusion of the *Moniage*. U is bounded by a broken line to suggest that we do not know its actual circumference; it is simply the "outside" and matters little where its boundries lie if indeed it has any. The process of the epic is to come to terms with A.

We know it is possible for there to be interaction between A and U, even for persons to move permanently from one space to the other (Rainouart, Guibourc). Once again the action of the epic appears to reduce itself to a binary function. Similarly, Karin M. Boklund has described the spatial and cultural world of the courtly romance as defined by two poles, in this case the *courtois* and the *vilain* ("On the Spatial and Cultural Characteristics of Courtly Romance" and "Socio-sémiotique du roman courtois"). Despite the risk of overreducing medieval texts, Boklund makes a reasonable case, and we are perfectly justified in representing the epic world as we have given the binary nature of it in other respects. What Boklund offers of real interest to the epic is to show that the romance world is nonmimetic, that it survives as a form of utopic fiction. The world of courtly romance, she says, is not a realistic one but one which gives form to a collective consciousness; it offers to the nobility a way of seeing the world and of acting upon it. In our terms, what Boklund is talking about is myth, and in fact some of what she says about the romance can be applied to the epic. It, too, is nonmimetic, and it certainly gives form to a collective consciousness and offers to a certain class a way of seeing the world and acting upon it. It succeeds in doing so partly because of its clear definition of its cultural and territorial spheres of influence. If the epic appears fuzzy about geography or topography this is not because spatial relationships are inconsequential to it. The essential spaces are rigorously guaranteed through yet another function of the familiar epic polarity.

Poet, Text(s), Interpreter

The types of space we have examined so far have been internal to the text itself, and yet there must be some sort of spatial relationship of a given text to entities exterior to itself. The text does not live, nor can it survive, by itself in a vacuum. A dynamic relationship exists between it, other texts, the poet, and certainly the interpreter. Much has been written about these textual concerns, theories of which are given such names as intertextuality and genidentity.

The intertextuality of the Guillaume epics is important not only because of the obvious relationships between poems but also because of the common base found in the various manuscripts of a given poem.[13] A network of "Guillaume-ness" exists both horizontally and vertically. The horizontal network is well known[14]; it is that which gives form to the poetic biography of the hero. The vertical network, which is atemporal, manifests the mythic aspects of the hero, and it is there that the total picture of the Cycle is given its identity. Here we see Guillaume, the beleaguered but steadfast knight, buoyed up by his wife (*Guillaume, Aliscans*), the ever-loyal knight in service to his king (*Couronnement*), the clever adventurer (*Prise, Charroi*), the mature and still loyal knight in a dual role as monk (*Moniage*). This image of Guillaume is built up in layers, but it is not the total picture of him.

Guillaume is not just Guillaume. He is a composite of relationships and characteristics held in common with other personnages in the text. He is the crudeness and ferocity of Rainouart, the nobility of Guibourc, the wisdom of Bertran (*Couronnement*), the patience of Landri (*Moniage*). The poet never embodies all of the characteristics of the hero in that one person but rather splits them among several just as the *Roland* poet has formed a "couple" in Olivier and Roland.[15] The interdependence of characters which necessarily links the various texts together, takes on spatial dimensions by virtue of its existence across boundaries of individual poems. Looking at the Guillaume Cycle from an intertextual point of view, the Cycle may be viewed as a hyper-text, a collectivity of that which is Guillaume and which in reality is incomplete if the whole is not taken as such.[16]

Yet Guillaume is not only the intertextual sum of characteristics taken from a collection of epic figures. He is genidentic with the whole range of themes, motifs, actions, semes, sememes, and mythemes that we have discussed. The concept of genidentity was put forth by Kurt Lewin in 1922 in his book entitled *Der Begriff der Genese*. More recently it has been discussed by Hans Reichenbach in *The Philosophy of Space and Time* and Joseph A. Kestner in *The Spatiality of the Novel*. Kestner's work is particularly useful despite the fact that it deals with a modern genre, for it applies what Lewin and Reichenbach have done for literature in general. Genidentity assumes a dynamic field of relationships and the possibility of individuals remaining identical across time. Reichenbach demonstrates this with a particle grid such as the following:

Figure IV

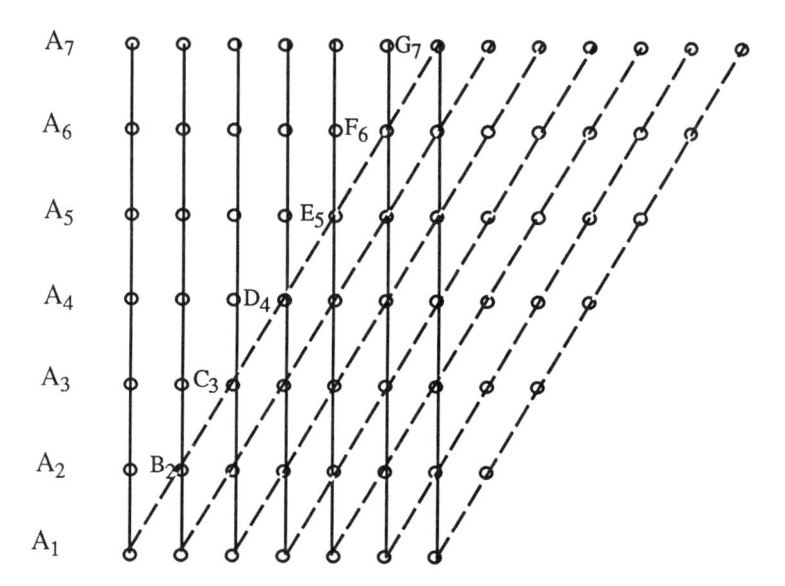

A1 may be seen as genidentical with A2, A3, and so on, as well as with B2, C3, D4, etc. With regard to literature, A and B may represent two texts and thereby show their individualities as well as their commonality. Likewise A1, B2, C3, and D4 may be personnages genidentic with one another. A1 may be a signifier while B2, C3, and D4 might be various signifieds of the sign. Or, A can be a text with B the interpreter of the text. The significance of this is that the experience of the literary text makes poet, text (or texts), and interpreter part of a dynamic spatial field. The problems of bridging the gaps between poet and text, text and interpreter, or poet and interpreter are therefore not problems at all, for there are no gaps to be bridged provided the three entities are genidentical with one another. The only problem lies in determining whether or not such a situation exists, but with respect to the epic this should not be a problem either. Without intending to beg the question, this genidentity could probably be said to exist if for no other reason than by virtue of the number of manuscripts produced; receptivity is a measure of the interpreter's identification with the art object. But beyond that, we have already demonstrated textually that a unified poetic consciousness existed for the Guillaume poems, a consciousness which generated multiple poems. Such generation and receptivity, as well as the common mythic underpinnings of the texts themselves, bear witness to the genidentic field in which poet, texts, and interpreters become genidentic with one another. This is another way of restating the theory that at the moment of interpretation the interpreter creates the text as a poet himself. The text, therefore, is in a constant state of generation or renewal, making the interpreters of a given moment genidentic with those of other times as well as with the "real" poet.

The text of a Guillaume poem is thus not a fixed entity—it is a living construction existing outside of time, given life by the only thing which can unite poet, text, and interpreter: language. Language gives shape and form to the text, that is to the conceptions of poet and interpreter, or it gives shape to the dynamic spatial field uniting the three. It is language which is the common consciousness of the text, the group spirit, the space occupied by poet, text, and interpreter. This is the genidentic space of the Guillaume Cycle poems where the myth is found in an harmonic, atemporal relationship with poet and interpreter.

Norris Lacy has suggested that the *chanson de geste* may be the most significant product of spatial composition in the Middle Ages.[17] The Guillaume poems certainly support any claim to spatial technique in the epic in view of their spatial framework, space modulation, and the dynamic spatial field encompassing poet, text, and interpreter. This brings us then to the real importance of epic spatiality.

In *The Spatiality of the Novel,* Kestner skillfully demonstrates how the essential function of certain modern novels is the manipulation of space and how, in particular, time becomes space in Proust's great novel. Kestner emphasizes that for Proust the search is not only for lost time but for space, noting the author's emphasis on "retrospection," "anticipation," "seeing again," and "after," whereby time is transformed into space through the genidentic process. Says Kestner, "The narrator, advising us not only how to create but to recreate, states: 'One must return backwards.' This is the novel that permits one to say: time regained is space" (161).

Now the Old French epic is hardly the modern novel, let alone the fact that it is hardly related substantively to *A la recherche du temps perdu*. The Guillaume Cycle is no less spatial, however, for it, too, is genidentic, "returns backwards," and turns time into space.

We have shown how it is genidentic by virtue of one text producing other texts by virtue of the intertextual dynamic field in which central figures are at once individual and multiple as well as by virtue of how themes, motifs, and the myth of Guillaume reproduce or recreate themselves from one text to another. This is to say that themes, motifs, the myth, and texts "return backwards." We are dealing here with the "myth of the eternal return."[18] We are now in the presence of a timeless world where what happens across time becomes spatial. "The acts of reading and of interpretation," says Kestner, "are...spatial and atemporal" (146). But, we can add that so is the process of composition to the extent that poet, text, and interpreter are all genidentic with one another. It would appear that this conversion of time into space would be in conflict with Bergson's notion that such cannot occur where duration is concerned, but in fact any durational state in the epic relies entirely upon the ability of the poet to create a spatial image or experience where only the *passage* of time (which, for Bergson, is spatial) does not occur or is not apparent. The Guillaume epic, with its emphasis upon spatial images and structure, genidentic relationships, and the constant recreation of the myth is an example of spatial art *par excellence*, and this, in fact, is consonant with Bergsonian duration: the epic, timeless present.

Let us return again to the basic question of myth. Ernst Cassirer demonstrated that "the intuition of space is a basic factor in mythical thinking, since this thinking is dominated by a tendency to transform all the distinctions which it postulates and apprehends into spatial distinctions and to actualize them in this form" (*The Philosophy of Symbolic Forms,* II, 94). In mythical thinking (and we affirm that this is true for mythical thought of any age, not just totemic societies) existence is perceived in classes, groups, and categories, that is, it is given spatial expression. Furthermore, says Cassirer, "The development of the mythical feeling of space always starts from the opposition of *day* and *night, light* and *darkness*" (96). Mythical thinking is dominated by antithesis, and this appears to be just as true for mythical thought embodied in artistic expression as well as religious expression. Of central concern to us, however, and this is again true for artistic as well as religious domains, is the perception of classes, groups, categories, and most especially antithetical constructions as a way of ordering one's experience with the world. This is not to say that this is the sole concern of mythical consciousness, but it is a crucial one, and it plays a dominant role in the consciousness of the Guillaume Cycle.

We know well of the chaotic period filled with wars, famines, pestilences and all manner of insecurity in which these poems were created and in which they circulated. It was a period in which man strove to find his identity or perhaps to create an identity. Guillaume represents the mythical consciousness in search of stability in the face of a chaotic environment, and he goes about this search in the most reliable, most effective way possible. He goes about it spatially.

Georges Matoré has said that time suggests death, that space suggests life:

> le temps, s'il est la matière de notre vie, est aussi et surtout la promesse de notre mort, l'espace est le milieu vital où s'incarne notre activité. Dans la pensé phénoménologique, l'appréhension de l'espace va permettre à l'homme d'éviter ce glissement sur les apparences, qui est pour lui un sujet d'angoisse, elle va l'aider à s'*ancrer* —à retrouver les *repères* et les *jalons* qui sont, dans certaines manifestations de la pensée d'aujourd'hui, les seuls points fixes qui surnagent de la pâte mouvante du réel. (*L'espace humain* 286-87)

But what Matoré says about the modern period is equally applicable to the Middle Ages, for Guillaume has shown us his compulsion to spatialize and to "s'ancrer." To do so is to give himself life and to give meaning to his world. Spatial concerns become permanent in periods of crisis.

One of the most important books in this century to have exercized an influence on criticism has been Wilhelm Worringer's *Abstraction and Empathy: a contribution to the psychology of style*. His influence has been most notable recently in Joseph Frank's *The Widening Gyre: crisis and mastery in modern literature*, a series of essays on spatial form in modern literature. Worringer was concerned with why, in the history of the plastic arts, there has been an alternation between naturalistic and non-naturalistic styles. What he noticed was that naturalistic styles appeared during the Greek classical period, the Italian Renaissance, and the art of Western

Europe up to the end of the nineteenth century. These were periods when the artist strove to represent nature and man as seen with the eye. In periods of non-naturalistic art—primitive art, Egyptian monumental sculpture, Byzantine and Romanesque art, and the artistic forms of the twentieth century—the artist concerns himself not with the treatment of space as he would in naturalistic styles, but rather with the plane, with linear-geometric forms. Organicism seems to lose to pure lines and forms. The essential difference for Worringer between these two basic styles had to do with the concept of *Kunstwollen*, or will-to-art, that is the type of form the artist desired his creation to take. In other words, there are good reasons for wanting a naturalistic or non-naturalistic style.

Worringer's explanation for the direction the will-to-art would take was this: naturalistic styles appeared in cultures which sensed an equilibrium between man and the cosmos, where man felt unified with and in control of his environment. Man thus enjoyed expressing his sense of harmony or oneness with the organic world. The non-naturalistic styles, however, reflect man's sense of chaos surrounding him. According to Worringer, the primitive would simply have no desire to represent this frightening spectacle in his art but would desire rather to reduce appearances of the natural world to simple forms having the stability, harmony, and sense of order he was looking for. As for later non-naturalistic periods, such as the Romanesque, Worringer believed that the culture dominated by religion so rejected the natural world as evil and imperfect that the will-to-art turned toward spiritualization and the suggestion of the ethereal and eternal through the dominance of the plane and linear-geometric patterns.

In order not to misrepresent him it is important to keep in mind that Worringer's thesis hinges upon a distinction between artistic styles which aim towards three-dimensional, corporeal space and those which opt for two-dimensional planar representations. There is "spatiality" in both styles. Yet several other important points must be considered here.

First, while Worringer explained the Romanesque will-to-art as a rejection of the natural world in favor of the ethereal on the basis of religious attitudes, this is an unsatisfactory explanation for the planar will-to-form in the epic. The consuming interest in the manipulation of space in the *chanson de geste*—which, as we have seen is not at all naturalistic—springs rather from the poet's desire to give shape and order to a chaotic environment. To use Worringer's term, the medieval poet may be more "primitive" than we usually admit.

Second, while we must remember that Worringer is talking about the plastic arts, what he says has proven to be equally valid for literature as Joseph Frank, himself, has demonstrated.

And, finally, the non-naturalistic style seeks to escape time, even, Frank says, in literature which is a "time-art." Worringer had argued that it is "space which, filled with atmospheric air, linking things together and destroying their individual closedness, gives things their temporal value and draws them into the cosmic interplay of phenomena" (38). But to that Frank has added, "Depth, the projection of three-dimensional space, gives objects a time-value because it places them in the real world in which events occur. Now time is the very condition of that flux and change from which, as we have seen, man wishes to escape when he is in a relation of disequilibrium with the cosmos; hence non-naturalistic styles shun the dimension of depth and prefer the plane.... In a non-naturalistic style, then, the inherent spatiality of the plastic arts is accentuated by the effort to remove all traces of time-value" (56-57).

What we can now see is that the tendency toward spatiality along with the concurrent removal of all traces of time-value is precisely what takes place in the Guillaume Cycle. There is narrative to be sure, and we cannot deny its own temporality in the sense of progression. Yet, the successful moments of duration, the dominant play with form and spatial relationships, the planar tableau-effect created by the poet, and above all the controlling factor of myth with all its attendant genidentic properties which, as we know, is by definition timeless (cf. Eliade, Cassirer), combine to spatialize these poems in a state of timelessness. It is in such a timeless state that both we and Guillaume achieve a sense of wholeness and order—wholeness and order out of polarity and chaos. The poems of the Guillaume Cycle are perfect examples of a time art which is largely rendered timeless. The whole notion of human work as a means to shaping one's environment according to his own image takes on mythic proportions by virtue of the high seriousness and universality of this idea, and this, in turn, demands the spatial, timeless framework the poet gives his art.

Chapter Six
The Final (Re)Turn

THE MYTH OF GUILLAUME DEALS WITH poetic and metaphysical truth. It is a response to the world and a prescription for an approach to the nature of things. It is a poetic statement about the condition of man confronted with the problems of creating an identity for himself and of finding means of dealing with a world in change and confusion. This is a myth about the process of integration which serves not to answer "why" or "from whence," but rather "how."

In the foregoing chapters we have examined the basic mythic consciousness of the *petit cycle* of Guillaume, the semiosis of this myth, and its spatio-temporal aspects. A number of observations have been made, certain of which are inescapable: Guillaume's major function is to come to terms with his environment metaphorically, to give it human proportions; the intertextual image of Guillaume looms large over the entire corpus as a symbol of the individual's struggle against the void in an effort to define his space in the world; and, the myth is ultimately spatial and atemporal with poet, text(s), and interpreter genidentic with one another, united in the textual experiential space of the poem. This image of Guillaume becomes, in fact, the central concern of the *petit cycle*. It reminds us of Lévi-Strauss's suggestion that "...it is likely that languages exist in which an entire myth can be expressed in a single word" (*Structural Anthropology*, II, 144). Indeed, Old French may be one such language, "Guillaume" one such word. The power of this word in the hand of the Guillaume poets is immense, for it is out of this word, innocuous at first, that the *gestes*, the poems, and the unity of the collection of texts are spun and to which everything in this corpus continuously and inevitably returns for significance. By the time the *petit cycle* is complete, the myth, wholly represented in the word, is itself complete and free to live on its own as if it no longer needed the poet at all. It is, as Lévi-Strauss, again, has said, that "myths grow spiritual-wise until the intellectual impluse which has produced them is exhausted" (*Structural Anthropology* I, 229).

Let us return a final time to the conclusion of the *Moniage Guillaume* and the curious whirlpool. We have already suggested that the whirlpool represents Guillaume's final victory over the chaos of his environment and the successful conversion of all unacceptable elements of his world into forces that he can dominate and control. It is nonetheless also the perfect ending to the cycle in terms of wholeness, completion, and the return to its source.

The whirlpool is a spiral, a spherical vortex which turns in and winds upon itself, creating a center and a "whole." In an interesting study entitled *The Mystic Spiral: journey of the soul*, Jill Purce states that "...vortical laws govern the movements of water which composes nearly three-quarters of our physical bodies. Water is the pure, potential and unformed matrix from which all life takes its being. Consequently, the characteristics of its vortical flow, its ephemeral but changeless configurations, remain in all things as a testimony of their origin" (8). She argues further that the spiral tendency within man is a longing for and growth toward wholeness, that every whole is cyclic with a beginning, middle, and end.[1] The spiral starts from a point, expands, differentiates, contracts, and disappears into the point once more. Furthermore, she remarks that with regard to classical labyrinths in particular, "The spiral movement...made chaos into cosmos and protected the holy space thus formed from illicit entry.... In classical times, the labyrinth, together with its ritual circumambulation, was essential to the creation of a city. This ritual imitated or re-enacted the original cosmic creation; for when a space is set aside or delineated it is ordered, carved out from the surrounding chaos, and so sanctified" (29).

The *Moniage* whirlpool stands as a hypersign of the *petit cycle* embodying the essentials of the myth of Guillaume as well as representing the spiral generation of it throughout the collection. It represents the final delimitation of space in this corpus of texts, the final transformation of chaos into form, and the achievement of total control, wholeness, and completion. It is also the final affirmation of the essential spatial and atemporal nature of the collection. The whirlpool, like the timeless epic present, will exist indefinitely as the pilgrims' symbol of the deeds of Guillaume just as its labyrinthine spiral endlessly turns upon itself and recalls the timeless efforts of human industry. Unlike classical times, perhaps, Guillaume's ritual circumambulation has not had as its focus the creation of the city but rather a more elemental reenactment of the original cosmic creation, the essential giving of shape and form to existence. Of all possible archetypal images, therefore, the *Moniage* justly ends on an image of water, what in effect has been the major controlling archetypal image throughout these poems, an image often found at the beginning of a new work-rest cycle. It stands as the origin of life, the source of renewal, the dissolution of evil. The *petit cycle*, like the whirlpool, turns in upon itself and reenters its point of origin as the myth of Guillaume takes on its final aspect at its moment of completion, the successful fulfillment of desire and ability through human work. Like the whirlpool, the myth, the image, and "the word" are also given permanent life in these waters now that they have become entirely spatial and atemporal. Guillaume does not die at the end of the *Moniage*—he is reborn as one complex mythic image embodying the universal truth of human effort to impose form on chaos. We can now understand why the myth "breaks down" to a large extent in most of the other poems in the larger, twenty-four-poem Cycle: the intellectual impulse has been "exhausted," satisfied in the closely unified *petit cycle*. There is simply no reason for it to be continued.

We have tried to examine the essential nature of the central poems of the Guillaume d'Orange Cycle, but many aspects of this poetry have been left untouched. We have said nothing about such things, for example, as tone, differences in language and style, the role of women, humor, irony, and paradox. Such aspects do not, however, influence the mythic coherence of the six closely related poems as we have viewed them. Yet the very fact of the *petit cycle* as something distinct from the remaining poems of the larger Cycle underlines one very significant question of enduring interest, and that is a clearer understanding, if not possible eventual generic definition, of the Old French epic. The epic may indeed have something to do with a burgeoning spirit of nationalism, the creation of a new French identity, or the elevation of certain social, political, and religious ethoi. All are elements to be found throughout the Cycle if not, perhaps, in all extant epics, but the tightly controlled myth of Guillaume as found in the *petit cycle* suggests, at the very least, that these elements do not adequately encompass the range of intentions of all epics. A definition of the genre will have to be dealt with elsewhere, however. Suffice it to say here that the myth of Guillaume considerably broadens the range of epic values that may be seen throughout the genre. It deals with what may not only be of significance to a society as a whole but with what is of central concern to the individual as he responds to his world, to "what is," or to "truth" as he sees it, and it does so in the only appropriate form—poetic form—that may adequately deal with an issue of such central human concern.

In the *New Science* Vico insisted that so-called "primitive" man responded to his world in a poetic manner, giving his responses to his environment in the form of metaphor, symbol, and myth. For Vico, a basic, human characteristic is the ability and necessity to generate myths, to deal with the world at one remove, or poetically. According to him, myth was a serious, cognitive way of dealing with reality, and for ancient peoples it was a means of representing their attempts to give a satisfying, humanizing form to their experience. Vico argued further that this form was born in the human mind and that it became the shape of the world which the mind thus perceived as "true." The *verum factum*, or what man perceived as true was also what he himself had made, one and the same, even if he were unaware of it. Man's perception is thus the shape of his own mind, or we might say that the world and the mind of such a man are genidentic with one another. Furthermore, said Vico, things are only "true" insofar as they can be made a part of the form which man's mind has given to the world. "...if we consider the matter well, poetic truth is metaphysical truth..." (74). Thus, myth is once again a statement about what is. And to the extent that man is the creator, the maker, the poet of what is, the only appropriate way in which to give shape and form to his vision of what is, is to do so poetically.

The poetic myth of Guillaume is thus a perfect response to the environment of man, an attempt to give humanizing form to experience where the experience itself and the form man attempts to give it are genidentic. Moreover, the mythic unity of the *petit cycle* is a singular artistic achievement, for the poetic consciousness of the myth, which transcends multiple authorship, and the spiral generation of these texts, a spiraling that mirrors Guillaume's ritual circumambulation, becomes inextricably fused in the image of Guillaume himself. The ultimate creation of this image, which is given its final form in the whirlpool scene, is not only artistically successful in coming to represent the complex of Guillaume's *gestes* along with the form, process, and significance of his struggle to give humanizing form to his experience in one spatial and timeless instant, but it is absolutely essential. Truth, the metaphysical truth of the world as man perceives it and as he expresses it in poetic myth for all men, is most perfectly expressed in a spatial, perdurable instant of time. The myth of Guillaume is just such a truth.

Notes

Chapter One

1. I take these poems to form the kernel of the larger cycle because they, together with the *Enfances Guillaume*, comprise the poetic biography of this epic hero. As indicated below, however, the *Enfances* was a late addition to the cycle intended to round out this biography and does not manifest the myth found in the six under discussion here.

2. Unless otherwise indicated, any reference to the *Moniage* will mean the *Moniage Guillaume II*, the longer of the two redactions.

3. Other poems examined included the *Chanson de Roland, Gormont et Isembard, Pèlerinage de Charlemagne, Moniage Rainouart, Foucon de Candie, Girart de Vienne, La Prise de Cordres et de Sebille, Le Siège de Barbastre, La Chevalerie Vivien, Raoul de Cambrai, Ami et Amile*.

Chapter Two

1. This definition and, indeed, much of what follows in this discussion of myth, is the result of considerable distillation of the writings of well-known scholars on the subject. Among them I am indebted to writers such as Lévi-Strauss, Barthes, Eliade, and Frye.

2. Emic terminology is characteristic of linguistics and semiotics and has to do with minimal, clearly distinct units of sound, form, or meaning. A phoneme, for example, is the smallest unit of sound that can be responsible for a difference in meaning and which, therefore, must have its

own identity or be clearly distinguishable from all other possible phonemes in a given language (e.g., the plural s in English). Moving up the "emic" ladder of complexity, the morpheme and lexeme are defined by minimal distinct differences in form and words respectively. The seme, which may be seen as more complex than the lexeme, has to do with qualities or characteristics. A group of semes are then responsible for defining a sememe which may be seen as something concrete or abstract having a particular meaning such as a knight errant. Finally, the mytheme, the most complex element in this system, is the minimal distinctive unit of significance necessary to a particular mythic framework; "knight errant Guillaume on a mission for Louis" in a particular poetic context would be an exemple of such a mytheme. More complete discussions of these distinctions may be found in Saussure (*Course in General Linguistics*), Greimas (*Sémantique structurale*), and Eco (*A Theory of Semiotics*).

3. The binary principle as a basis for meaning is well known and has been discussed widely in fields such as linguistics, literature, and anthropology. See, for example, Saussure or Lévi-Strauss.

4. These terms and the process of semanticization are fully explored in Eco and Greimas.

5. The terms "apocalyptic" and "demonic" as well as the definition of civilization used in this study are taken from Frye. The structure derived from the Guillaume poems is mine.

6. It is generally acknowledged that the *Chanson de Guillaume* consists of two major parts, the first ending at verse 1980. See Wathelet-Willem's edition for a full discussion of this problem.

7. In his edition of the *Moniage*, Cloetta discusses the possible sources of the allegorical garden episode extending back as far as Herodotus and Titus-Livius. See pp. 148-51.

8. The devil as bridge-builder is a common German and Scandinavian folklore motif. There is also at least one case where the devil destroys by night a bridge that humans attempt to build by day. See Wünsche 30.

Chapter Three

1. Note Barthes's hesitation about binarism in *Elements of Semiology* 80-82 where he emphasises that the universality of binarism is not yet founded and therefore not certain.

2. An excellent discussion of these concepts may be found in Gérard Genette's "Frontières du récit." *Communications* 8 (1966): 152-63.

3. Propp's study of the Russian folktale led him to isolate thirty-one possible functions which could be used to compose a text. I believe that from the point of view of functions the epic is a much simpler genre on the whole. I also feel that the archetypal structural analysis presented here offers considerably more in terms of interpretation of these texts. As for Greimas, while his actantial analysis, particularly involving the use of a semiotic square, may offer an interesting look at the relationships between characters, their relationships to various situations, and consequently an understanding of the meaning of the texts, I am not convinced that the Guillaume epics will fit neatly into his schemes or offer us as much as what I propose to show here.

4. It is clear that characters are not actants, but since I do not intend to pursue actantial analysis, and since I believe that for an understanding of the semiosis of the myth we must deal with specific characters in specific contexts, I have opted for the former term.

5. Much of the *Chanson de Roland* tends to be imagistic in this way with its constant shifting from one character or isolated combat scene to the other.

6. See Greimas's comments on this problem in *Sémantique structurale* 30-31.

7. We might say that there are no circumstantial distinctions or that this context obviates the need for such a division since all circumstances in which we find *destrier* are the same regardless of whether we are talking about a Frankish *destrier* or a Saracen one.

8. cf. Kristeva. *Le texte du roman* 133.

9. cf. Kristeva 69-72.

10. cf. Kristeva 122-23.

11. As Kristeva points out with respect to the *Jehan de Saintré*, "Dans [le contexte des combats chevaleresques], tout autre discours (le commerce, la foire, les vieux livres, la cour) passe au second plan et ne peut être que qualificatif: il n'a pas 'la force' de transformer un actant (nominal) en un syntagme narratif verbal, donc, il n'a pas la force de former un récit" (*Le texte du roman* 123).

12. On this point see Leyla Perrone-Moises, "L'intertextualité critique." *Poétique* 27 (1976): 372-84.

Chapter Four

1. de Romilly, *Time in Greek Tragedy*, provides an excellent discussion of this subject.

2. See: Richard Glasser, *Time in French Life and Thought* ; M. H. A. Blanc, "Time and Tense in Old French Narrative," and "Le présent épique dans la *Chanson de Roland* "; Minette Grunmann, "Temporal Patterns in the *Chanson de Guillaume* "; Anna G. Hatcher, "Tense Usage in the *Roland,* " and "Epic Patterns in Old French: A Venture in Stylistics via Syntax"; Lucien Foulet, *Petite syntaxe de l'ancien français*; Léopold Peeters, "Le *faire* et le *dire* dans la *Chanson de Roland,* " and "Le présent épique dans la *Chanson de Roland* "; Rupert T. Pickens, " Historical Consciousness in Old French Narrative"; Paul Imbs, *Les propositions temporelles en ancien français: la détermination du moment. Contribution à l'étude du temps grammatical français*; Friederike Stefenelli-Fürst, *Die Tempora der Vergangenheit in der Chanson de Geste*; Imre Szabics, "Procédés expressifs dans le *Charroi de Nîmes.* "

3. Pickens defines the historical tenses as preterites, imperfects, and pluperfects, the "present" tenses as presents and perfects.

4. I have not followed Pickens's approach absolutely, for he identifies a third or commentative (authorial intervention) part of a text. I have chosen to include commentary as part of diegesis for the sake of simplicity. In any case, commentary usually accounts for only about 1 percent of the text.

5. See his Table I, p. 171.

6. See especially Blanc's "Time and Tense in Old French Narrative" and "Le présent épique dans la *Chanson de Roland.*"

7. An example of this is v. 1767 of the *Couronnement* where *baise* will not satisfy the meter, and so *baisa* has to be used. This does not change any effect which might be obtained in using the preterite, however.

8. Note that I have accepted Wathelet-Willem's correction in verse 133 of *vestent to vestirent*.

9. This work is given an excellent analysis by Shlomith Rimmon in "A Comprehensive Theory of Narrative; Genette's *Figures III* and the Structuralist Study of Fiction."

10. See also other prayers in *Chanson de Guillaume* 897-912; *Aliscans* 546-62, 567-84, 5254-62, 7076-7119; *Couronnement de Louis* 695-789, 976-1029; *Moniage Guillaume* 1681-1704, 2010-20.

11. There are other possibilities in Genette's schema, but they are inappropriate here.

12. Related questions on the perspective of the past in the epic are taken up in a series of works by Stephen G. Nichols, Jr.: "The Interaction of Life and Literature in the *Peregrinationes ad Loca Sancta* and the Chansons de Geste"; "Poetic Reality and Historical Illusion in the Old French Epic"; "The Spirit of Truth: Epic Modes in Medieval Literature"; and, *Romanesque Signs: early medieval narrative and iconography*. See also Eugene Vance, "Roland et la poétique de la mémoire."

Chapter Five

1. Gérard Genette discusses some general types of literary spatiality in his essay entitled "La littérature et l'espace" in *Figures III*.

2. Much has been written about the Guillaume poems in attempting to pin down specific historical events, their location, and the supposed sites of events in the poems. A perennial question seems to be the exact location of "Archamps" in the *Chanson de Guillaume*. André de Mandach's "Le 'Fragment de la Haye' et le site des 'campi strigilis' " and Jeanne Wathelet-Willem's *Recherches sur la chanson de Guillaume* adequately summarize this question to date. As for the other poems in the Cycle the most recent editions as well as Jean Frappier's *Les chansons de geste du cycle de Guillaume d'Orange* offer a good introduction to problems of historicity and localization.

3. Jean-Charles Payen has pointed out that in the epic, space (as well as time) is easily molded to fit the modalities of combat, and that the inconsistency and deformation of the epic landscape show how certain areas take importance with regard to a particular theme. See "Encore le problème de la géographie épique." Similar views are found in H. S. Kay, "Topography and the Relative Realism of Battle Scenes in *Chansons de Geste*."

4. Norris Lacy has also demonstrated how the epic poet—in this case of the *Roland*—is capable of exploiting "visual possibilities of narration to produce effects of intensity, variety, and suspension." See "Roland at Roncevaux: The Poet's Visual Art."

5. Eugene Vance ("Roland et la poétique de la mémoire") and Stephen G. Nichols, Jr. ("Sign as [Hi]story in the *Couronnement de Louis* " and *Romanesque Signs: early medieval narrative and iconography*) have both discussed the importance of the sign in the epic. Vance points out how society leans toward a "metaphysics of the sign" in expressing a need to commemorate Roland after his death, "to render vivid the *hic et nunc* of the lived." Nichols shows how the sign of Guillaume's nose is a symbol for his and God's power and influence against the infidel. He emphasizes

further that in the epic the world must be exhaustively interpreted as a symbol of divine immanence.

6. On this point see particularly Fern Farnham, "Romanesque Design in the *Chanson de Roland*." Farnham states that Romanesque (plastic) art disdains both space and time in favor of an experience of transcendence—a view to which I cannot subscribe totally given the de-emphasis on space here. Yet she correctly emphasizes the extra-temporal nature of this period of art, including literature: "Centrality, symmetry, paratactic structure, insistence upon a supra-temporal which, for all its magnificence, cannot rob the temporal of its vigor—all this is characteristic of the age and can be found in the tympanum at Moissac, in the *Saint Alexis*, and, most triumphantly, in the *Roland*" (164).

7. Other views on retrospection, retrogression, and echoing in medieval literature may be found in Stephen G. Nichols, Jr., "The Rhetoric of Recapitulation in the *Chanson de Guillaume*"; Norris J. Lacy, "Spatial Form in Medieval Romance"; D. D. R. Owen, "Structural Artistry in the *Charroi de Nîmes*."

8. For a discussion of ring composition in the *Iliad* see Cedric Whitman, *Homer and the Heroic Tradition*.

9. As for Type II, there are seventeen occurrences in G1 and twenty-two in G2.

10. For the probable history of the development of the extant MS, see Jeanne Wathelet-Willem's *Recherches sur la Chanson de Guillaume*.

11. Alfred Adler has expressed the view that Guillaume's purpose in the *Couronnement* was the defense of the Holy Roman Empire, not just France. See "The Dubious Nature of Guillaume's Loyalty in the *Couronnement de Louis*."

12. In *Medieval French Literature and Law*, R. Howard Bloch argues that the effectiveness of the feudal system is called into question in the epic as a means of settling conflicts and disputes. His case is convincing, although the Guillaume Cycle is given short shrift in making

global statements about the Old French epic. In the main we do not see this cycle as struggling with the problems of feudal practice quite the way the rebel baron cycle or even the *Roland* does.

13. For a discussion of the manuscripts in the cyclic tradition see Madeleine Tyssens's *La geste de Guillaume d'Orange dans les manuscrits cycliques*.

14. e.g., Frappier's study of the *petit cycle*; in *Les chansons de geste du cycle de Guillaume d'Orange*.

15. See particularly Gerard J. Brault's *The Song of Roland*.

16. On general problems of intertextuality see Laurent Jenny, "La stratégie de la forme"; Julia Kristeva, *Le texte du roman: approche sémiologique d'une structure discursive transformationnelle*; Juri Lotman, *La structure du texte artistique*; Michael Riffaterre, *Semiotics of Poetry*.

17. Lacy's view that the *chanson de geste* may be the most significant product of spatial composition in the Middle Ages is based upon the paratactical development of this poetry by means of the juxtaposition of blocks of material. He points out that the poet typically shows less interest in establishing links of temporal or causal sequence than in constructing the individual scene (338-39).

18. cf. Mircea Eliade, *Le mythe de l'éternel retour*.

Chapter Six

1. Kestner makes a similar comment. In speaking of Flaubert's *Education sentimentale* he states that the spiral is the image of form and that life, emerging from shells, reaches into its past (*The Spatiality of the Novel* 62).

Bibliography of Works Cited

Editions

Aliscans. Kritischer Text von Erich Wienbeck, Wilhelm Hartnacke, Paul Rasch. Halle: Max Niemeyer Verlag; 1903.

Le Charroi de Nîmes: chanson de geste du XIIe siècle. J.-L. Perrier, ed. Paris: Champion; 1967 (Classiques Français du Moyen Age).

Le Couronnement de Louis: chanson de geste du XIIe siècle. Ernest Langlois, ed. Paris: Champion; 1966 (Classiques Français du Moyen Age).

Les deux rédactions en vers du Moniage Guillaume: chansons de geste du XIIe siècle publiées d'après tous les manuscrits connus. Wilhelm Cloetta, ed. 2 tomes. Paris: Firmin-Didot; 1906, 1911 (Société des Anciens Textes Francais).

La Prise d'Orange; chanson de geste de la fin du XIIe siècle, éditée d'après la rédaction AB avec introduction, notes et glossaire. Claude Regnier, ed. 2ème ed. Paris: Klincksieck; 1969 (Bibliothèque Française et Romane; Série B: Editions critiques de Textes).

Wathelet-Willem, Jeanne. *Recherches sur la Chanson de Guillaume: études accompagnées d'une édition.* 2 tomes. Paris: Société d'Edition "Les Belles Lettres"; 1975 (Bibliothèque de la Faculté de Philosophie et Lettres de l'Université de Liège; 210).

Critical Studies

Adler, Alfred. "The Dubious Nature of Guillaume's Loyalty in *Le Couronnement de Louis.*" *Symposium.* 1948; 2: 179-94.

——. *Epische Spekulanten. Versuch einer synchronen Geschichte des altfranzösischen Epos.* Munich: Fink; 1975 (Theorie und Geschichte der Literatur und der schönen Kunste; Band 33).

——. "Guillaume, Vivien, et Rainouart: le souillé et le pur." *Romania.* 1969: 1-13.

——. "Rainouart and the Composition of the *Chanson de Guillaume.*" *Modern Philology.* 1951; 49: 160-71.

Andersson, Theodore M. *Early Epic Scenery: Homer, Virgil and the Medieval Legacy.* Ithaca: Cornell University Press; 1976.

Bachelard, Gaston. *La poétique de l'espace.* Paris: Presses Universitaires de France; 1957.

Barthes, Roland. *Elements of Semiology.* tr. Annette Lavers and Colin Smith. New York: Hill and Wang; 1968.

——. "An Introduction to the Structural Analysis of Narrative." *New Literary History.* 1975; 6 (2): 237-72.

Bartsch, H. *Sagen, Märche und Gebraüche aus Mecklenburg.* I: 400 (number 555) [reported in Wünsche—see below].

Becker, Philipp Auguste. *Das Werden der Wilhelm—und Aimerigeste: versuch einer neuen Lösung.* Leipzig: Hirzel; 1939 (44 Bandes, Der Abhandlung der philologisch—historischen Klasse des sachsischen Akademie der Wissenschaften. Nr. I.).

Bédier, Joseph. *Les légendes épiques: recherches sur la formation des chansons de geste.* 4 volumes. 3ème ed. Paris: Champion; 1926.

Bergin, Thomas Goddard and Max Harold Fisch. *The New Science of Giambattista Vico: revised translation of the third edition (1744)*. Ithaca: Cornell University Press; 1968.

Bergson, Henri Louis. *Essai sur les données immédiates de la conscience*. Paris: Alcan; 1932.

Blanc, Michel. "Le présent épique dans *La Chanson de Roland*." *Actes du Xe Congrès International de Linguistique et Philologie Romanes, Strasbourg 1962*. volume 2. Paris: Klincksieck; 1965. 565-78.

——————. "Time and Tense in Old French Narrative." *Archivium Linguisticum*. 1964; 16: 96-124.

Blanchot, Maurice. *L'espace littéraire*. Paris: Gallimard; 1955.

Bloch, Marc. *Feudal Society*. 2 volumes. Chicago: University of Chicago Press; 1961.

Bloch, R. Howard. *Medieval French Literature and Law*. Berkeley: University of California Press; 1977.

Boklund, Karin M. "On the Spatial and Cultural Characteristics of Courtly Romance." *Semiotica*. 1977; 20 (1/2): 1-37.

——————. "Socio-sémiotique du roman courtois." *Semiotica*. 1977; 21 (3/4): 227-56.

Brault, Gerard J. *The Song of Roland: an analytical edition*. 2 volumes. University Park: The Pennsylvania State University Press; 1978.

Bremond, Claude. *La logique du récit*. Paris: Seuil; 1973.

Calin, William C. *The Old French Epic of Revolt: Raoul de Cambrai, Renaud de Montauban, Gormont et Isembard*. Geneva: Droz; 1962.

Cassirer, Ernst. *The Philosophy of Symbolic Forms, II. Mythical Thought.* tr. Ralph Manheim. New Haven: Yale University Press; 1955.

Corti, Maria. *An Introduction to Literary Semiotics.* tr. by Margherita Bogat and Allen Mandelbaum. Bloomington: Indiana University Press; 1978.

Crist, Larry S. "Remarques sur la structure de la chanson de geste: *Charroi de Nîmes—Prise d'Orange.*" *Charlemagne et l'épopée romane; actes du VIIe Congrès International de la Société Rencesvals, Liège, 28 août—4 septembre 1976.* II. Liège: Université de Liège; 1978. 359-72.

Curtius, Ernst Robert. *Europaische Literatur und lateinisches Mittelalter.* Bern: 1945.

—————. "Über die altfranzösischen Epik." *Zeitschrift für romanische Philologie.* 1944; 64: 233-320; and, *Romanische Forschungen.* 1950; 62: 294-349.

Eco, Umberto. *A Theory of Semiotics.* Bloomington: Indiana University Press; 1976.

Eliade, Mircea. *Le mythe de l'éternel retour: archétypes et répétition.* Paris: Gallimard; 1949.

Falk, Eugene H. *Types of Thematic Structure: the nature and function of motifs in Gide, Camus, and Sartre.* Chicago: University of Chicago Press; 1967.

Farnham, Fern. "Romanesque Design in the *Chanson de Roland.*" *Romance Philology.* 1964; 18: 143-64.

Foulet, Lucien. *Petite syntaxe de l'ancien français.* 3ème éd. rev. Paris: Champion; 1977.

Frank, Joseph. *The Widening Gyre: crisis and mastery in modern literature.* New Brunswick: Rutgers University Press; 1963.

Frappier, Jean. *Les chansons de geste du cycle de Guillaume d'Orange.* 3 volumes. Paris: Société d'Edition d'Enseignement Supérieur; 1955, 1967, 1983.

Frye, Northup. *Anatomy of Criticism: four essays.* New York: Atheneum; 1968.

Genette, Gérard. *Figures I, II, III.* Paris: Seuil; 1966, 1969, 1972.

—————. "Frontières du récit." *Communications.* 1966; 8: 152-63.

Glasser, Richard. *Time in French Life and Thought.* tr. C. G. Pearson. Totowa: Rowman and Littlefield; 1972.

Greimas, A. J. *Sémantique structurale.* Paris: Larousse; 1966.

Grunmann, Minette. "Temporal Patterns in the *Chanson de Guillaume.*" *Olifant.* 1976; 4 (1): 49-62.

Hatcher, Anna Granville. "Epic Patterns in Old French: A Venture into Stylistics via Syntax." *Word.* 1946; 2 (1): 8-24.

—————. "Tense Usage in the *Roland.*" *Studies in Philology.* 1942; 39: 597-624.

Holman, C. Hugh. *A Handbook to Literature.* 3rd ed. New York: Bobbs-Merrill; 1972.

Imbs, Paul. *Les proportions temporelles en ancien français: la détermination du moment. Contribution a l'étude du temps grammatical français.* Strasbourg: Publications de la Faculté des Lettres de l'Université de Strasbourg; 1956.

Jakobson, Roman and Morris Halle. *Fundamentals of Language.* The Hague: Mouton; 1956.

Jeanroy, Alfred. "Etudes sur le cycle de Guillaume au court nez. II. *Les Enfances Guillaume, Le Charroi de Nîmes, La Prise d'Orange*; rapport de ces poèmes entre eux et avec *La Vita Willelmi*." *Romania*. 1897; 26: 1-33.

Jenny, Laurent. "La stratégie de la forme." *Poétique*. 1976; 27: 257-81.

Jonckbloet, Wm. J. A. *Guillaume d'Orange: chansons de geste des XIe et XIIe siècles*. La Haye: 1854.

Kay, H. S. "Topography and the Relative Realism of Battle Scenes in *chansons de geste*." *Olifant*. 1977; 44: 259-78.

Kestner, Joseph A. *The Spatiality of the Novel*. Detroit: Wayne State University Press; 1978.

Kristeva, Julia. *Le texte du roman: approche sémiologique d'une structure discursive transformationnelle*. The Hague: Mouton; 1970.

Lacy, Norris J. "Roland at Roncevaux: The Poet's Visual Art." *Rocky Mountain Modern Language Association Bulletin*. 1972; 26 (1): 3-8.

———. "Spatial Form in Medieval Romance." *Yale French Studies*. 1974; 51: 160-69.

———. "Spatial Form in the 'Mort Artu'." *Symposium*. 1977; 31 (4): 337-45.

Lévi-Strauss, Claude. *Mythologiques; le cru et le cuit*. Paris: Plon; 1964.

———. *Structural Anthropology*. vol. 1 tr. by Claire Jacobsen and Brooke Grundfest Schoepf; vol. 2 tr. by Monique Layton. New York: Basic Books; 1963, 1976.

Lewin, Kurt. *Der Begriff der Genese*. Berlin; 1922.

Lessing, Gotthold Ephraim. *Laocoon: an essay on the limits of painting and poetry*. tr. Edw. Allen McCormick. New York: Bobbs-Merrill; 1962.

Lotman, Juri M. *La structure du texte artistique*. Traduit du russe par Anne Fournier, Bernard Kreise, Eve Malleret et Joelle Yong sous la direction d'Henri Meschonnic. Paris: Gallimard; 1973.

McLuhan, Marshall and Harley Parker. *Through the Vanishing Point*. New York: Harper and Row; 1968.

de Mandach, André. "Le 'Fragment de la Haye' et le site des 'campi strigilis'." *Charlemagne et l'épopée romane: actes du VIIe Congrès International de la Société Rencesvals, Liège, 28 août— 4 septembre 1976*. II. Liège: Université de Liège; 1978. 617-28.

Matoré, Georges. *L'espace humain: l'expression de l'espace dans la vie, la pensée et l'art contemporains*. Paris: La Colombe; 1962.

Meyerhoff, Hans. *Time in Literature*. Berkeley: University of California Press; 1960.

Nichols, Stephen G., Jr. "The Interaction of Life and Literature in the *Peregrinationes ad Loca Sancta* and the Chansons de Geste." *Speculum*. 1969; 44: 51-77.

———. "Poetic Reality and Historical Illusion in the Old French Epic." *French Review*. 1969; 43: 23-33.

———. "The Rhetoric of Recapitulation in the *Chanson de Guillaume*." *Studies in Honor of Tatiana Fotitch*. Washington: Catholic University Press; 1972. 79-92.

———. *Romanesque Signs: early medieval narrative and iconography*. New Haven: Yale University Press; 1983.

———. "Sign as (Hi)story in the *Couronnement de Louis*." *Romanic Review*. 1980; 71 (1): 1-9.

———. "The Spirit of Truth: Epic Modes in Medieval Literature." *New Literary History.* 1970; 1 (3): 365-86.

Niles, John D. "Ring Composition in *La Chanson de Roland* and *La Chançun de Willame.*" *Olifant.* 1973; 1 (2): 4-12.

Owen, D. D. R. "Structural Artistry in the *Charroi de Nîmes.*" *Forum for Modern Language Studies.* 1978; 14: 47-60.

Payen, Jean-Charles. "Le *Charroi de Nîmes,* comédie épique?" *Mélanges de langue et de littérature du Moyen Age et de la Renaissance offerts à Jean Frappier, professeur à la Sorbonne, par ses collègues, ses élèves et ses amis* vol. II. Genève: Droz; 1970. 891-902.

———. "Encore le problème de la géographie épique." *Société Rencesvals IVe Congrès International, Heidelberg, 28 août— 2 septembre 1967. Actes et mémoires.* Heidelberg: Carl Winter; 1969. 261-66 (Studia Romanica; 14).

Peeters, Leopold. "Le *faire* et le *dire* dans la *Chanson de Roland.*" *Revue des Langues Romanes.* 1975; 81: 376-93.

———. "Le présent épique dans la *Chanson de Roland.*" *Revue des Langues Romanes.* 1975; 81: 399-423.

Perrone-Moises, Leyla. "L'intertextualité critique." *Poétique.* 1976; 27: 372-84.

Pickens, Rupert T. "Historical Consciousness in Old French Narrative." *French Forum.* 1979; 4 (2): 168-84.

Poulet, Georges. *La distance intérieure.* Paris: Plon; 1952.

———. *Etudes sur le temps humain.* Paris: Plon; 1949.

Propp, Vladimir. *Morphology of the Folktale.* First edition translated by Laurence Scott with an introduction by Svatava Prikova-Jakobson. Second edition revised and edited with a preface by Louis A.

Wagner. New Introduction by Alan Dundes. Austin: University of Texas Press; 1968.

Proust, Marcel. *A la recherche du temps perdu.* 3 vols. Paris: Gallimard; 1954 (Bibliothèque de la Pléiade).

Purce, Jill. *The Mystic Spiral; journey of the soul*. London: Thames and Hudson; 1974.

Quinones, Ricardo. *The Renaissance Discovery of Time.* Cambridge: Harvard University Press; 1972.

Reichenbach, Hans. *The Philosophy of Space and Time.* tr. Marie Reichenbach and John Freund. New York: Dover; 1958.

Riffaterre, Michael. *The Semiotics of Poetry.* Bloomington: Indiana University Press; 1978.

Rimmon, Shlomith. "A Comprehensive Theory of Narrative; Genette's *Figures III* and the Structuralist Study of Fiction." *Journal for the Study of Poetics and the Theory of Literature.* 1976; 1 (1): 33-62.

de Romilly, Jacqueline. *Time in Greek Tragedy.* Ithaca: Cornell University Press; 1968.

Saint Augustine. *Confessions.* tr. Vernon J. Bourke. Washington: Catholic University Press; 1953.

de Saussure, Ferdinand. *Course in General Linguistics.* ed. by Charles Bally and Albert Sechehaye in collaboration with Albert Riedlinger; translated, with an introduction and notes by Wade Baskin. New York: McGraw-Hill; 1959.

Stefenelli-Fürst, Friederike. *Die Tempora der Vergangenheit in der Chanson de Geste.* Stuttgart: Wilhelm Braumuller, Universitäts-VerlagsBuchhandlung Ges M. B. H.; 1966. (V. Band. Wiener Romanistische Arbeiten. Wien IX/66).

Szabics, Imre. "Procédés expressifs dans le *Charroi de Nîmes*." *Annales Universitatis Scientiarum Budapestinensis de Rolando Eötvos nominatae.* Sectio Philologica moderna. 1973; 4: 22-36.

Thornton, Harry and Agathe. *Time and Style; a psycholinguistic essay in Classical literature.* (in collaboration with A. A. Lind). London: Methuen; 1962.

Tindall, William York. *The Literary Symbol.* Bloomington: Indiana University Press; 1955.

Todorov, Tzvetan. "Les categories du recit litteraire." *Communications.* 1966; 8: 125-51.

―――――. *Grammaire du Décameron.* The Hague: Mouton; 1969.

Tyssens, Madeleine. *La geste du Guillaume d'Orange dans les manuscrits cycliques.* Paris: Société d'Edition "Les Belles Lettres"; 1967 (Bibliothèque de la Faculté de Philosophie et Lettres de l'Université de Liège; 178).

Uitti, Karl. *Old French Narrative Poetry: story, myth, celebration.* Princeton: Princeton University Press; 1973.

Uspensky, Boris A. "Structural Isomorphism of Verbal and Visual Art." *Poetics.* 1972; 5: 5-39.

Vance, Eugene. "Roland et la poétique de la mémoire." *Cahiers d'études médiévales.* 1975; 1: 103-15.

―――――. "Spatial Structure in the *Chanson de Roland.*" *Modern Language Notes.* 1967; 82: 604-23.

Vico, Giambattista. *The New Science*; see Bergin, Thomas Goddard.

Wathelet-Willem, Jeanne. *Recherches sur la Chanson de Guillaume; études accompagnées d'une édition.* 2 vols. Paris: Société d'Edition "Les Belles Lettres"; 1975 (Bibliothèque de la Faculté de Philosophie et Lettres de l'Université de Liège; 210).

Weinrich, Harald. *Le temps: le récit et le commentaire.* traduit de l'allemand par Michele Lacoste. Paris: Seuil; 1973.

Whitman, Cedric. *Homer and the Homeric Tradition.* Cambridge: Harvard University Press; 1958.

Worringer, Wilhelm. *Abstraction and Empathy: a contribution to the psychology of style.* New York: International Universities Press; 1953.

Wünsche, August. *Der Sagenkreis vom Geprellten Teufel.* Leipzig und Wien: Akademischer Verlag; 1905.

Zumthor, Paul. *Essai de poétique médiévale.* Paris: Seuil; 1972.

———. "Intertextualité et mouvance." *Littérature.* 1981; 11: 8-16.

Index

Adler, A., 3, 4, 101, 125
Aliscans, 1, 5, 20, 22-27, 28, 39, 47-48, 49, 50, 53, 70, 72, 73, 76-77, 78, 79, 80, 81, 94, 95, 101, 103, 105, 123
Ami et Amile, 119
anachrony, 78-79
Andersson, T., 92
anisochrony, 78, 79, 81, 82
apocalyptic imagery, 12-19, 120
appositional mode, 82-86
Aymeri de Narbonne, 5

Bachelard, G., 88
Barthes, R., 36, 38, 39, 119, 121
Bataille Loquifer, 5
Becker, P.-A., 3
Bédier, J., 3, 4
Beowulf, 92, 94, 95
Bergson, H., 62, 64, 68, 108
binarism. *See* opposition, principle of
Blanc, M., 122, 123
Blanchot, M., 88
Bloch, M., 63, 66
Bloch, R., 125
Boklund, K., 104
Brault, G., 126
Bremond, C., 36, 38

Calin, W., 66, 91
Cassirer, E., 108, 111

Chanson de Guillaume, 1, 3-4, 5, 20-22, 24, 25, 47, 49, 50, 53, 66, 70, 72, 73, 74, 76, 77, 78, 79, 80, 84, 91, 94, 95, 96-97, 98, 100, 101, 103, 105, 120, 123, 124
Chanson de Roland, 7, 8, 65, 66, 92, 94, 95, 105, 119, 121, 124, 126
characters, 38-39, 40, 50, 51, 52
Charroi de Nîmes, 1, 5, 20, 27-28, 29, 49, 50, 54, 58, 70, 72, 73, 79, 81, 95, 102, 103, 105
Chevalerie Vivien, 119
circumstance, 44-50
civilization goal, 12, 19
Cloetta, W., 120
connotata, 44-50
context, 44-50
Corti, M., 58
Couronnement de Louis, 1, 4-5, 11-19, 20, 21, 22, 28, 49, 58, 70, 72, 73, 75-76, 78, 79, 80, 82, 91, 93, 95, 102, 103, 105, 123, 125
Crist, L., 3
Curtius, E., 3, 91

demonic imagery, 12-19, 120
denotata, 44-50
Doon de Mayence Cycle, 1, 126
duration, 62, 64, 68, 73-77, 78, 79, 80, 81, 82-86, 108, 111

Eco, U., 36, 43, 58, 120
Eliade, M., 111, 119, 126
emic terminology, 8, 9, 119
encounters, 38-39, 40, 42, 50, 52-56
Enfances Guillaume, 5, 119

Falk, E., 10
Farnham, F., 125
Foucon de Candie, 119
Foulet, L., 122
Frank, J., 109, 111
Frappier, J., 4, 5, 99, 124, 126
frequency, 78, 80
Frye, N., 32, 119, 120

Genette, G., 37-38, 39, 67, 78, 80, 88, 121, 123, 124
genidentity, 104-11, 113, 116
genotext, 52
Gilgamesh, 7, 8
Girart de Vienne, 119
Glasser, R., 64, 65, 122
Gormont et Isembard, 66, 119
Greimas, A., 36, 38, 43, 51, 120, 121
Grunmann, M., 122

Hatcher, A., 122
Herodotus, 120
histoire, 78-80
Holman, H., 10
hypersign, 56, 58, 114
hyper-text, 105

image, 9, 10, 115; archetypal, 11-33, 37, 42-43, 45, 50, 52, 59, 60, 115; mythic, 41, 56, 57, 58, 60
Imbs, P., 122
In Honorem Hludowici, 92
intertextuality, 2, 53, 56, 57, 59, 60, 105, 113, 126
intratextuality, 56

Jeanroy, A., 2
Jenny, L., 57, 126
Jonckbloet, W., 4

Karolus Magnus et Leo Papa, 92
Kay, H., 124
Kestner, J., 105, 107, 108, 126
King Cycle, 1
Kristeva, J., 36, 37, 59, 122, 126

Lacy, N., 107, 124, 125, 126
Lessing, G., 87-88
Lévi-Strauss, C., 37, 101, 113, 114, 119, 120
Lewin, K., 105, 106

lexeme, 10, 44, 120
Lotman, Y., 59, 126

McLuhan, M. and Parker, H., 89
macrotext, 56, 58, 59
de Mandach, A., 124
Matoré, G., 109
metonymy, 36
Meyerhoff, H., 63
Moniage Guillaume, 1, 5, 20, 26, 29-33, 39, 47, 50, 54, 56, 58, 70, 72, 73, 78, 79, 80, 81-82, 91, 93, 95, 102, 103, 104, 105, 114, 115, 119, 120, 123
Moniage Rainouart, 119
morpheme, 10, 11, 120
Mort Aymeri de Narbonne, 5
motif, 10, 35, 105
myth, 7-11, 35, 115, 116; emic level, 9; narrative level, 8-9; syntagmatic/paradigmatic level, 9
mytheme, 10, 11, 40, 41, 42, 91, 105, 120
Mwindo epic, 7, 8

Narbonnais, Les, 5
narration, 36-38; diegesis, 37-42, 47, 48, 69, 70-73; mimesis, 37, 40, 41-42, 69, 70-73; paradigmatic features, 36-37, 40-41, 42, 43, 56; syntagmatic features, 36-41, 43, 56
Nichols, S., 123, 124, 125
Niles, J., 94

Odyssey, 82, 94
Oedipus, 7
opposition, principle of, 35, 36, 39, 41, 42, 43, 46, 50, 52, 57, 121
Owen, D., 125

Payen, J.-C., 93, 124
Peeters, L., 122
Pèlerinage de Charlemagne, 119
Perrone-Moises, L., 122
phenotext, 52
phoneme, 10, 11, 43, 119
Pickens, R., 69, 71, 73, 122, 123

Poulet, G., 64, 88
Prise de Cordres et de Sebille, 119
Prise d'Orange, 1, 5, 20, 27, 28-29, 46-47, 54, 58, 70, 72, 73, 78, 79, 81, 82, 92, 95, 102, 105
Propp, V., 38, 51, 121
Proust, M., 62, 79, 107
Purce, J., 114

Quinones, R., 64

Raoul de Cambrai, 66, 119
récit, 78-80
Reichenbach, H., 105, 106
Renaud de Montauban, 66
Riffaterre, M., 126
Rimmon, S., 123
ring composition, 94-95
Roman de Renart, 93
de Romilly, J., 122
rules of action, 51, 52-54

St. Augustine, 62
de Saussure, F., 120
seme, 10, 40, 43, 44-50, 52, 90, 105, 120
sememe, 10, 40, 44-50, 90, 105, 120; animate, 48, 50; archetypal, 45-46, 50; human, 48-50; nonarchetypal inanimate, 46-48, 50
semiosis, 35-60
Siège de Barbastre, 119
signs, iconic, 39-41, 42, 56; indexical, 39-41, 42, 56
situations, 51
space modulation, 96-104
spatial framework, 90-95
Stefenelli-Fürst, F., 69, 122
supersign, 58
symbol, 9, 10
Szabics, I., 122

temporal distortion, 78-80

temporal formulas, 80-81
temporal markers, 81-82
tenses, 69-77
theme, 9-10, 105
Theseus, 7
Thornton, H. and A., 82-84
Titus-Livius, 120
Todorov, T., 36, 38
Tyssens, M., 2, 5, 126

Uitti, K., 65
Uspensky, B., 89

Vance, E., 92, 123, 124
Vico, G., 116
Virgil, 92

Waltharius, 92
Wathelet-Willem, J., 3, 4, 120, 123, 124, 125
Weinrich, H., 67
Whitman, C., 125
work/rest cycle, 11-19
Worringer, W., 109-111
Wünsche, A., 120

Zumthor, P., 2, 65